About the author

Peter Marsden has a degree in Modern Arabic and worked for a number of years as a Middle East specialist before undertaking further training in community development. He spent fifteen years in poverty and health programmes in the UK and then returned to his previous focus on the Islamic world while drawing on his community development experience to move into the overseas aid field. For the past thirteen years he has worked as Information Coordinator of the British Agencies Afghanistan Group, in which role he has provided information to NGOs, UN agencies, donors, the media and academics on humanitarian needs in Afghanistan and on the wider political, economic and cultural context. He has undertaken extensive research on Afghanistan and is a Research Associate of Queen Elizabeth House, Oxford.

This book is an extensively updated and expanded edition of the author's previous book, *The Taliban*, taking into account the wholly new context in which Afghanistan and its people find themselves in the wake of the terrorist bombing of the World Trade Center in New York on September 11, 2001.

The Taliban: War and Religion in Afghanistan

Peter Marsden

Spearhead CAPE TOWN
Forum Books KUALA LUMPUR
Manohar Publishers NEW DELHI
The University Press DHAKA
Vanguard Books LAHORE
White Lotus BANGKOK
Zed Books Ltd
LONDON • NEW YORK

The Taliban: War and Religion in Afghanistan was first published by Zed Books Ltd, 7 Cynthia Street, London N1 9JF, UK and Room 400, 175 Fifth Avenue, New York, NY 10010, USA in 2002.

Distributed exclusively in the United States by Palgrave, a division of St. Martin's Press, LLC, 175 Fifth Avenue, New York 10010, USA.

Published in Bangladesh by The University Press Ltd, Red Crescent Building, 114 Motijheel C/A, PO Box 2611, Dhaka 1000
ISBN 984 05 1621 3

Published in Burma, Cambodia, Laos and Thailand by White Lotus Company Ltd, GPO 1141 Bangkok 10501, Thailand.
ISBN 974-4800-04-6 paperback

Published in Ghana by EPP Book Services, PO Box TF490, Trade Affairs, Accra.

Published in India by Manohar Publishers, 4753/23 Ansari Road, Darya Ganj, New Delhi 110 002.
ISBN 81 7304 446 5 paperback

Distributed in Indonesia by ak.'sa.ra, PT Panaksara Pustaka, Jalan Kemang Raya 8b, Jakarta 12730.

Published in Pakistan by Vanguard Books, 45 The Mall, Lahore.

Published in South Africa by Spearhead, a division of New Africa Books, PO Box 23408, Claremont 7735.
ISBN 0 86486 524 4 paperback

Maps reproduced from *Afghanistan: A Nation of Minorities* © Minority Rights Group 1992

Cover designed by Andrew Corbett
Set in Monotype Baskerville and Univers Black by Ewan Smith
Printed and bound in the United Kingdom by Biddles Ltd, Guildford and King's Lynn

A catalogue record for this book is available from the British Library.

ISBN 1 84277 166 3 cased
ISBN 1 84277 167 1 limp

Contents

Chronology

BC

522–330   Afghanistan subject to Achaemenid empire of Darius the Great and his successors.

330–327   Alexander the Great conquers Afghanistan.

AD

64–220   Afghanistan subject to Kushan dynasty. Development of the Silk Route.

224–651   Afghanistan subject to Sasanian dynasty and Hephthalite empire.

699–700   Islamic conquest of Afghanistan. Hindu Shahi and other dynasties continue as vassals of the Ummayad Caliphs based in Damascus.

977–1186   Ghaznavid dynasty, based in Ghazni, creates empire stretching from Isfahan to north-west India.

1155–1227   Genghis Khan wreaks destruction over Central Asia and the wider region.

1370–1506   Afghanistan subject to Timurid dynasty.

1506–1747   Afghanistan split between Moghul and Safavid empires.

1747–72   Ahmed Shah Durrani conquers Afghanistan from Kandahar.

1809   Britain signs a treaty of mutual defence with the Afghan Amir against Russia and France.

1839–42   First Anglo-Afghan war.

1878–80   Second Anglo-Afghan war. Treaty of Gandamak in 1879 provides that Britain will control Afghanistan's foreign affairs.

1880–1901   Abdur-Rahman undertakes comprehensive conquest of Afghanistan and establishes Pushtun populations in the north. Present boundaries of Afghanistan fixed through a series of international agreements.

1901–19   Habibullah rules Afghanistan.

1919–29	Amanullah rules Afghanistan. Treaty of Rawalpindi in 1919 provides that Afghanistan free to conduct its own foreign affairs. Reform movement attempted but meets massive backlash from religious and traditional leadership.
1929	January–October: Bacha-e-Saqqao, a Tajik, rules from Kabul.
1929–33	Nadir Shah, a Pushtun, replaces Bacha-e-Saqqao and rules at behest of tribal and religious leadership.
1933–73	King Zahir Shah rules under guidance of his uncles and then of his cousin and prime minister, Daoud, until asserting his independence following resignation of Daoud in 1963. Constitution of 1964 provides legal equality for men and women and sets in motion a period of political unrest and growing radicalism.
1973	July: King Zahir Shah overthrown by Daoud through a military coup.
1978	April: People's Democratic Party of Afghanistan takes power through a military coup.
1979	December: Soviet troops invade Afghanistan.
1989	February: Soviet troops withdraw from Afghanistan.
1992	April: Mujahidin government takes power in Kabul.
1994	November: Taliban capture Kandahar.
1995	September: Taliban capture Herat.
1996	September: Taliban capture Jalalabad and Kabul.
1997	May: Abortive attempt by the Taliban to capture Mazar-i-Sharif in the north.
1998	August: Taliban capture Mazar-i-Sharif. USA launches air strikes on Afghanistan in reponse to the terrorist attacks on the US embassies in Nairobi and Dar es Salaam.
1999	October: UN Security Council imposes sanctions on the Taliban.
2000	September: Taliban capture Taloqan in the north-east.
	December: UN Security Council imposes further sanctions on the Taliban.
2001	September: Terrorist attack on World Trade Center and the Pentagon. Osama bin Laden held responsible by the USA.
	October: USA with British support launches air strikes and bombing raids on Afghanistan. The war begins.

Map 1 Afghanistan and neighbouring states

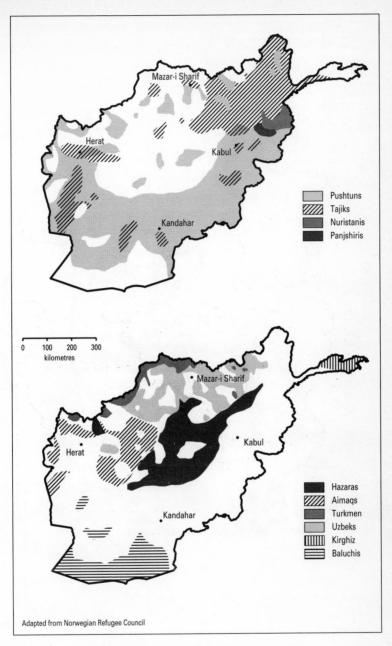

Mazar-i Sharif

Herat

Kabul

Kandahar

Pushtuns
Tajiks
Nuristanis
Panjshiris

0   100   200   300
kilometres

Mazar-i Sharif

Herat

Kabul

Kandahar

Hazaras
Aimaqs
Turkmen
Uzbeks
Kirghiz
Baluchis

Adapted from Norwegian Refugee Council

Map 2 Major ethnic groups of Afghanistan

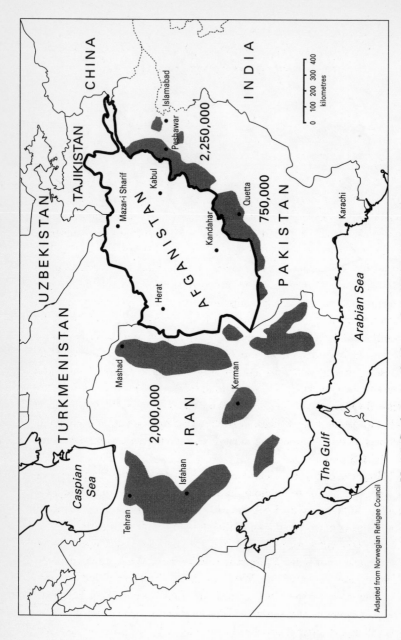

Map 3 Settlements of refugees from Afghanistan, January 1992

Adapted from Norwegian Refugee Council

Preface: the Difficult Questions in the Wake of September 11

The terrorist attacks on the World Trade Center and the Pentagon on Tuesday September 11, 2001 have brought into focus the nature of the relationship between the West and the Islamic world. The attacks have raised a number of important questions. Were they a consequence of particular policies pursued by the USA in the Islamic world and, if so, would a reversal of such policies be the most effective means of protecting the West from future terrorist attacks? Notable among the negative US policies cited was its support for the repressive policies of Israel towards the Palestinians, the consistent bombing of Iraq, the continued US military presence in Saudi Arabia and the Gulf, the air strikes against the Sudan and Afghanistan of August 1998 and the subsequent UN sanctions against Afghanistan of October 1999 and December 2000. The US response to the attacks, in which it immediately named Osama bin Laden as the prime suspect, raised the question of whether he, and the Taliban in Afghanistan by association, were being scapegoated so that the US government could present a concrete enemy to the US public.

However, one of the clear conclusions of this book is that there is no shortage of people throughout the Islamic world who share Osama bin Laden's antipathy to the USA and who would be capable of orchestrating sophisticated terrorist attacks. If, therefore, one accepts the premise that Osama bin Laden is simply one among many who could have planned the attacks, what is the appropriate way forward? What are the choices? Is it the case, as many in the West fear, that the military action begun in October 2001 by the USA against the Taliban and alleged terrorist training camps in Afghanistan will produce another generation of terrorists willing to martyr themselves for the cause. Would it be the case that, however many Taliban supporters and supporters of Osama bin Laden were killed by US forces in battle, many thousands more would volunteer to take their place? Would terrorist attacks on Western targets increase? Or would such attacks occur in any event for so long as, for example, the USA maintains a military presence in Saudi Arabia? If the USA and its allies were to use Pakistani soil for a full-scale invasion of Afghanistan, would this radicalise the population of Pakistan to the point where the present regime of Pervez Musharraf was replaced, through a coup, by a radical Islamic one with access to Pakistan's nuclear arsenal? Could the USA prevent such an outcome? If it had a military presence in Pakistan, would it be able to protect the present regime against a coup attempt? Would it have the wherewithal to strengthen Pakistan's capacity to weaken the radical parties within its borders? How difficult would this be when a significant element in both the Pakistan military and Pakistan's intelligence services are likely to be sympathetic to the Taliban and to Osama bin Laden? How easy would it be for the USA to penetrate Osama bin Laden's network, referred to as Al-Qaida? To what extent is Osama bin Laden the supreme organiser as opposed to an inspirational force, a symbol of opposition to US foreign policy? If, as many state, Al-Qaida is an extremely loose network of people sharing a common vision and acting relatively independently of each other, can the USA locate the parts of the network where future terrorist attacks are being planned? If these are identified and disabled, will other cells emerge to carry out the same or similar attacks?

There are other even more strategic questions. If the international community concludes that the only way forward to ensure the long-term security of the planet is to abandon the 'crusade' mentality and engage more constructively with the Islamic world, what is the purpose of such engagement? Is it to win over moderates within the Islamic world or isolate the extremists? Should the international community be leaving the responsibility to individual governments to deal with extremists within their own borders? There are, after all, Islamic radicals within Europe as well as in Islamic countries. Do Muslim radicals living in Europe and North America have greater potential to carry out terrorist attacks against Western targets than those trained in the alleged terrorist training camps in Afghanistan? If the USA, instead of using Pakistan as a base for incursions into Afghanistan, were to encourage Pakistan to locate and prosecute, through the courts, extremists within its own borders, would the Pakistani population accept this? Similarly, if the USA had used the same standard of proof, in demanding the extradition of Osama bin Laden by the Taliban, as they would have had to provide in extradition proceedings elsewhere in the world, would the Pakistani and Afghan publics have acknowledged that justice had taken its course and have assented to the action taken? If, at the same time, the USA were to persuade Israel to abandon its settler policy and its repressive approach towards the Palestinian population, would this win over moderate opinion within the Islamic world? If the USA were to cease all aggressive military action against the Islamic world, would attitudes towards the USA soften? If the USA were to accept that it should apply the same standards in considering military intervention in an Islamic state as it would in considering such action against a European state, would this make a difference to how the USA is perceived in the Islamic world? Or has the USA so alienated Muslim opinion through its military action in Afghanistan and its arrogant disregard of their sentiments that the USA will remain an object of intense hatred for some time to come? Does military action against Afghanistan represent the most effective use of resources in seeking to tackle terrorism? Would the USA seriously contemplate invading Britain, for example, if it had suspicions that the attacks on the World Trade Center and the Pentagon had been organised from there? Or would it trust the UK to take what action it could to use the legal framework of the country to bring the suspects to justice? Can the USA justify having departed from such a principle in relation to the Taliban? What are its criteria? What is it about the Taliban that makes the USA feel that it has the right to set aside normal international principles of engagement between one governing entity and another?

This book seeks to reflect on many of the questions raised above and on the dilemmas that inevitably arise. The starting point, however, has to be Afghanistan itself. This is the country that the USA attacked militarily, starting in October 2001 – and this despite not a single Afghan having been identified as a suspect in the terrorist attack on the World Trade Center and the Pentagon. Nor is it the first time that the USA has bombed this utterly impoverished and war-wrecked country; former President Bill Clinton launched cruise missile attacks on Afghanistan back in August 1998, again because of allegations that Osama bin Laden was involved in the destruction of the US embassies in Nairobi and Dar es Salaam that year. It is therefore in Afghanistan that we must begin any serious attempt to explore the very important and difficult questions raised above. We have to try to understand the course of events inside that tragic country, how it was that radical Islamic forces became so powerful, why the particular faction called the Taliban eventually took power, what they believe, and how this set in motion a chain of events that has resulted in the current war. Understanding the Taliban, and Afghanistan more generally, is what this book is about.

1 Introduction

This book is about relationships: between the West and the Islamic world, between the various movements in the Islamic world and within Afghanistan, and between the people of Afghanistan as they respond to the experiences that have overwhelmed them since the 1978 coup and the subsequent Soviet invasion. It is an attempt to understand a picture that becomes ever more complex the more one pursues its various strands. The Taliban are but one manifestation of the impact of the Afghan conflict but they bring into focus a web of factors spanning the interface between Islam and Christianity, developments within Islam as a religion and as the basis for a political ideology, international power politics and the international economy. Every effort to clarify the situation raises further questions, and there are no easy labels with which to define the Taliban.

However, when they took Kabul at the end of September 1996, and – whether by design, accident or as an act of revenge quite independent of the Taliban – ex-President Najibullah and his brother were hanged in a public square, the image they presented was stark and simple. Their subsequent declarations banning female access to education and employment, their imposition of strict dress codes on both women and men, and their dramatic military conquests brought to the surface all the negative stereotypes about Islam that have beset both international relations and race relations within Europe.

The high level of media attention and the punitive approach the Taliban adopted towards the population of Kabul made it difficult for the international community to avoid taking a stance. However, both they and the international agencies were made keenly aware of the evident popularity of the Taliban in many of the areas they had conquered, even though their popularity in Kabul was far from assured. It was therefore impossible to go for outright condemnation and a severing of relations. A way had to be found of engaging in dialogue in the hope that policies that were more consistent with international norms could be negotiated.

This book is one among many efforts to facilitate this process, by seeking to establish, as much as can reasonably be achieved within a book of this size, an objective understanding of the current situation. It therefore looks at what the Taliban believe and how this set of beliefs has manifested itself in the different parts of Afghanistan and in relation to different elements in the population. It also, very tentatively, explores the many possible influences, both cultural and religious, that appear to have fashioned Taliban policies and their implementation. In order to do this one has to look at the wider geopolitical picture and at Afghanistan's role in the world economy, and to take on board the country's ethnic, religious and linguistic mix and the nature of its terrain. All these have influenced the behaviour of the Taliban.

Similarly, their behaviour has generated a set of responses among Afghanistan's neighbours as well as in the West, with potentially conflicting agendas operating within each neighbouring state. These agendas have included the very considerable interests relating to Afghanistan's role as a major producer of opium, its direct involvement in the processing of heroin, its potential as a conduit for Central Asian gas and oil and its heavy involvement in smuggling.

It is also important to consider the major problems the Taliban movement has created. How, for example, should the international community respond to abuses of human rights, such as the denial of female access to education and employment, in considering issues such as international recognition? How should it compare this abuse with the extreme forms of physical abuse committed by many governments that have been accorded international recognition? Should it take a stricter stand in relation to physical abuse, worldwide? How should humanitarian agencies respond to human rights abuse?

In seeking to engage and negotiate with a movement such as the Taliban, what benchmarks should one be using? Are the UN Human Rights Conventions appropriate or are they, as the Taliban state, based on Western value systems? Should one take the view that radical movements can be a symptom of the state of a society and that one should respect their philosophies as a manifestation of popular belief, or should one look to the views of moderates and liberals within the population to guide one's negotiating position? Should one be influenced by what Islamic scholars are saying as to what is or is not consistent with the Qur'an and the reported sayings of the Prophet Muhammad, the Hadith? Should one look to women within the population of Islamic scholars and other intellectuals to indicate what may be reasonable norms? Alternatively, should one draw on the perspectives and values of those living in the rural areas of Afghanistan, both women and men? In so doing, how does one take on board the diversity of perspectives and values from village to village, province to province and one ethnic group to another?

Even if one establishes appropriate benchmarks, one is still dealing with a movement that contains people with a range of perspectives and attitudes. Some within the movement may respond positively to negotiations that demonstrate an acceptable level of sensitivity, while others may be reluctant to negotiate at all. Faced with this inevitable internal divergence, the international community has often felt at a loss in assessing whether the Taliban have been responding positively to negotiations on human rights issues. It has often seemed that, with every apparent move forward, there has been a negative incident that has seriously soured international attitudes. That problem is not, of course, unique to Afghanistan, but it is one that has to be addressed.

The question of how the international community should respond to human rights abuses in a conflict situation is a complex one. During the Soviet occupation, from 1979 to 1989, there was a tendency to criticise the abuses of the occupying forces because they were seen as the unprovoked aggressor, and to turn a blind eye to abuses committed by the Mujahidin, who, at that time, were accorded the image by the media of heroic freedom-fighters. When the Soviet troops withdrew and the abuses committed by the Mujahidin continued (albeit on a smaller scale, with the exception of one or two major episodes), it was felt that these could be dismissed as the inevitable consequence of a highly factionalised civil war. It was only when the Taliban took Kabul and asserted themselves as the government of Afghanistan, by virtue of the fact that they controlled two-thirds of the country, that the question of whether they should adhere to international norms became a major issue. Their previous capture of Herat, another liberal and cultured city, had aroused no more than a flicker of international concern.

It has been necessary to engage with the Taliban on a number of fronts. Primary among these, in terms of the frequency of interaction, has been the need for humanitarian agencies to negotiate authority to operate in Taliban-controlled areas and to achieve access to all sections of the population and to all parts of the country, including those held by the opposition. However, the hospitality accorded to Osama bin Laden by the Taliban has, since the US air strikes of August 1998, taken much greater prominence on the international stage and has led to a fierce debate within the international community as to the balance to be aimed at between coercion and constructive engagement in tackling this issue. The Taliban have responded within an Islamic framework to demands from the USA that Osama bin Laden be handed over in connection with charges that he was involved in the bombings of the US embassies in Nairobi and Dar es Salaam. This, combined with the heroic status that the subsequent air strikes accorded to Osama bin Laden, has meant that actions taken by the international community, and particularly by the USA, in response to this issue have been presented as confrontational with the Islamic world. It is thus evident that the air strikes and the subsequent UN sanctions imposed on the Taliban to put pressure on them to hand over Osama bin Laden have had the effect of strengthening the hardliners within the Taliban and radicalising the political environment within neighbouring Pakistan through a strengthening of the Islamic parties. There are many, however, who argue that this confrontational and denunciatory approach has proved to be counterproductive and that a policy of more constructive engagement with the Taliban should be pursued. This book endeavours to inform a consideration of this dilemma even if it cannot offer easy solutions. It is hoped that it will also contribute one more voice to the long-standing debate on the interface between the Islamic world and the West.

The book starts by setting the scene, noting Afghanistan's geographical characteristics, its ethnic, religious and linguistic mix, the nature of its economy, the complexities of its culture and its history. It then moves on, in Chapter 3, to a consideration of the Mujahidin movement and its manifestations both in and out of government. This is crucial to an understanding of the Taliban and of the relationship between humanitarian agencies and the Taliban.

Chapter 4 examines the origins of the Taliban and the nature of its leadership, and follows the dramatic events that led to the Taliban capture of Kabul and the subsequent efforts to take northern Afghanistan. It assesses the impact of the Taliban on the different populations under their control, and explores the reasons for the considerable divergence between one area and another.

Chapters 5 to 7 are an attempt to identify what I have described as the Taliban creed. My own conclusion, from studying the many statements Taliban leaders have made and from looking at their actions, is that, while they have a clear set of beliefs, there is no theoretician providing a written framework to guide the movement as it finds its way forward. There does not, therefore, appear to be what one might term an ideology. Rather there is a creed, to which there is clearly a passionate allegiance that appears to draw on a large number of influences.

Chapter 5 outlines the nature of the creed, largely as defined by the Taliban in their public statements. Chapter 6 looks at other radical movements that have risen to prominence in the Islamic world, namely those of the Muslim Brotherhood, the Wahhabis in Saudi Arabia, Gaddafi's Libya and the Iranian Revolution, to enable us to identify more clearly the characteristics of radical Islamic movements that are present in the Taliban and those that are lacking. Chapter 7 goes back to the eighteenth century in the Indian subcontinent to trace the evolution of Islam within it, and particularly within Afghanistan, to reflect on the possible influences on the Taliban. This chapter considers the debate that continues to dominate among observers as to how far the Taliban creed draws on custom and practice among the Pushtun tribes and how far it draws on the thinking of the religious establishment within Afghanistan, on the ideologies of the Islamist parties within the Mujahidin and on leading theoreticians in the subcontinent, notably the highly conservative Abdul Ala Maududi.

Chapter 8 considers what is perhaps the most difficult issue in the relationship with the Taliban, that of gender, and considers how Taliban policies have affected both women and men. Any effort to tackle this subject has to get to grips with what may be regarded as normal custom and practice in Afghanistan. This is not easy. There have been considerable variations over time and between one part of Afghanistan and another, and the conflict has complicated the situation enormously.

We have also to look at the position of women within Islam and in relation to the norms pertaining in the different parts of the Islamic world, covering the spectrum from liberalism to radical Islam. We have, at least, to consider how far the Taliban interpretation of Shari'a law, of the Qur'an and of the Hadith, is consistent with the prevailing understanding by Islamic scholars, even though we do not question the right of the Taliban to make their own interpretations. It is of equal importance to clarify the nature of gender-related thinking in the West if we are to engage in a realistic debate. In so doing, the chapter notes the gender-specific provisions of the UN Human Rights Conventions and considers how far these represent value systems within both the West and the Islamic world.

This brings us, in Chapter 9, to the dialogue with the humanitarian agencies. This chapter considers the impact of the Taliban on the work of the agencies, the nature of the dialogue between them and the problems raised both by this dialogue and by the human rights abuses that have punctuated the discussions. It looks at the responses of agencies to developments and at the attempts by agencies to identify appropriate benchmarks for the dialogue.

Chapter 10 examines the interface between the Taliban and the international community, by which is meant the diplomatic community of the UN Security Council, the European Community and individual governments considering the question of diplomatic recognition. It considers the statements made by the UN, the European Union and certain governments, explores the issues raised and relates these to a consideration of human rights issues globally. It also tentatively explores the attitudinal difficulties in the relationship between Christianity and Islam, dating back to the crusades, and the often pronounced prejudice on both sides that colours the relationship.

Having delved deeply into comparative value systems, the book jumps into the world of *realpolitik* to examine the global and regional interests that affect the relationship of the Taliban to the outside world. Chapter 11 considers the apparent support for the Taliban by elements within Pakistan, while Chapter 12 looks at the wider region, notably the factors that have led Russia, Iran, Tajikistan and India to take up positions opposed to the Taliban and caused Turkmenistan to stand on the sidelines. This leads to an exploration of the gas and oil pipelines story and of the Taliban position on heroin, smuggling and terrorism.

Chapter 13 recounts briefly the long relationship Osama bin Laden has had with Afghanistan and the Taliban. The concluding chapter stresses the wider significance of the Taliban and their enduring conflict with the USA, including the options that now exist for relations between the West and radical Islam after 11 September.

2 The Nature of Afghanistan

In a country like Afghanistan, where the concept of the nation has developed but recently, where the state is seen as external to society and where people's allegiance is directed primarily towards the local community, the only thing which all Afghans have in common is Islam (Roy, 1986: 30).

Afghanistan can be characterised geographically as a mountainous desert interspersed with isolated fertile valleys, river basins and oases. It extends eastward from the vast Iranian plateau and incorporates the foothills of the Himalayan range, which rise to a height of 7,470 metres in the finger of land that divides Tajikistan from Pakistan and touches on western China. To the north of this range, known as the Hindu Kush, begin the plains that cross the Afghan frontier at the Amu Darya river and stretch for thousands of miles across Central Asia and the Russian steppes to the Arctic. To the south of the Hindu Kush is a bleak and windswept desert that passes through Pakistan to the Indian Ocean. Archaeological evidence indicates that people were growing wheat and barley and grazing sheep and goats on the foothills of the Hindu Kush some 9,000 to 11,000 years ago. It also suggests a strong nomadic culture over the wider region to the west and north.

The economy is based almost exclusively on subsistence agriculture, with irrigated wheat as the major crop. Rainfed wheat and barley are grown on the more marginal land. The conflict with the Soviet Union led to the neglect or destruction of many of the irrigation structures on which the agricultural economy has depended, and much of the aid provided in recent years has been aimed at their repair. The years since the departure of Soviet troops have therefore witnessed an effective restoration of the agricultural base, as people have returned to their villages after external or internal exile. The process of reconstruction has been assisted by the resources and engineering skills provided by humanitarian agencies. Until the serious drought that commenced in 2000, the rural economy was showing an improvement, at least in the south and west of the country, but parts of the north were showing a continuing deterioration.

Certain areas have fared much better than others. The area around Jalalabad, for example, is able to produce a wide range of fruit and vegetables. In addition, until the ban on opium production imposed by the Taliban, which took effect in 2001, it was well known for its poppy production. Helmand, which was the other main poppy-growing area, provided one-quarter of the world supply. Jalalabad is also situated astride a major trade route and acts as the centre of a highly organised smuggling network. By contrast, the river valleys of central and north-eastern Afghanistan, the length of the Hindu Kush, barely ensure survival and have a history of famines, some of major proportions.

The conflict has seen a mushrooming of Afghanistan's urban centres as a proportion of the population have opted to move to the towns and cities in an effort to survive economically. The subsidies provided by the Soviet Union kept the urban economy reasonably buoyant until 1992, but the events since then have resulted in a steady decline. There has been a process of families gradually selling off their possessions over the years and many are now facing destitution. The urban economy has always relied heavily on small workshops and on street trading, both highly vulnerable to instability or fear of arrest.

The people of Afghanistan are ethnically, religiously and linguistically mixed. The dominant ethnic group, the Pushtuns, inhabit the southern part of the country in an arc circling the Hazara area of central Afghanistan. There are as many Pushtuns on the Pakistan side of the border, in North-West Frontier Province, as on the Afghan side. The Pushtuns have a distinct language, Pashto, which is significantly different from Dari, a dialect of Persian spoken in other parts of the country.

In the north of the country there are three main ethnic groups, which link with others of the same ethnic affiliation in Central Asia. The small Turkoman population in Badghis province thus relates to Turkmenistan, the much larger Uzbek population in the north central region, centred on Mazar, to Uzbekistan, and the Tajiks of north-eastern Afghanistan to Tajikistan. The Uzbeks and Turkomans are

Turkic in origin and Turkey has shown a particular interest in them of late, as part of its pan-Turkic ambitions in Central Asia. Yet another ethnic group, the Baluch, are to be found in the south-western corner of Afghanistan as part of a wider population on both the Pakistani and Iranian sides of the border.

Sunni Islam is the dominant faith but there are two significant Shi'a minorities: the Hazaras of central Afghanistan, who have historically been marginalised both politically and economically, and the Ismailis of north-eastern Afghanistan. Eighty per cent of the population are Sunni and 20 per cent Shi'a (Roy, 1986: 30).

Culturally, the country is very mixed. The Pushtun belt is tribal and highly traditional, with clearly defined codes of conduct governing relationships within the family and with outsiders to the tribe. The consensual system of decision making characteristic of Afghanistan is particularly pronounced in the Pushtun areas. The local structures, known as *jirgas*, which are to be found in the Pushtun belt have played a major role in the maintenance of the societal fabric. The *shuras*, which exist in other parts of Afghanistan, are much looser in their hold.

The Shi'a Hazara population of central Afghanistan may also be described as conservative, but the codes of behaviour are less rigid than those of the Pushtun south. The society is, in addition, quite hierarchical and individualistic. It is not uncommon for women to have to bring up children on their own within a system where the nuclear rather than the extended family is dominant. Similarly, in the northwest, around Herat, the population before the war was noted to be extremely mobile as nuclear families moved from place to place in search of work. In Mazar, the population is even more urban in character and could be regarded as having more in common with the inner-city areas of Western conurbations than with the very traditional south. However, the rural areas around it are not significantly less conservative than the Pushtun belt, although they lack the cohesion that exists in the Pushtun areas. It is therefore much easier for the area to fragment into warring factions of varying affiliations.

The capital, Kabul, has moved through many stages as the city has espoused modernism, reverted to ultra-traditionalism, been influenced by the liberalism of the 1960s, adopted the outward manifestations of Soviet-style socialism and seen its liberal intelligentsia depart in waves in the face of purges and the arrival of, first, the People's Democratic Party of Afghanistan (PDPA) regime, which took power in 1978, the Mujahidin government of 1992–96, and, more recently, the Taliban government. With the pronounced move to the cities that has resulted from the conflict, the capital is, in many ways, now more rural than urban in character.

It is difficult to determine whether Afghanistan belongs more appropriately in Central Asia, in the Indian subcontinent or in the Middle East. The tribal culture of the Pushtuns bears many similarities to that of the Arabian peninsula, yet the system of purdah that is so characteristic of Muslim society in south Asia is also in evidence. The enigma is compounded by the impact on the various cultures and sub-cultures within Afghanistan of the conflict following the Soviet invasion. No one has been unaffected by the conflict, but it has inevitably been more traumatic for some than for others. More than six million people fled into exile, most to Iran and Pakistan but many to Europe, North America and India. Large numbers have been displaced within the country, some spending the war in caves in the mountains, others seeking sanctuary in the cities or in other parts of the country. Exile has exposed people to other cultures but it has at the same time increased their defences to outside influences. Thus women in exile have been more constrained in their mobility than is the norm within Afghanistan. It is more appropriate to consider Afghanistan as a place of enormous complexity that has been subject to a constant state of flux throughout history rather than to view it as somehow caught in a time-warp, with life going on as it has always done.

Historically, Afghanistan has been inextricably linked with Iran and Central Asia by virtue of its position astride the ancient trade route between Europe and China, with the fortunes of the Indian subcontinent periodically linked with those of Afghanistan. Yet it was always somewhat apart from its neighbours, its population hiding away in isolated valleys, fiercely defending their independence while remaining, to an extent, dependent on the trade generated by the outside world. Its geography has made it a perfect centre for smuggling, with borders impossible to patrol effectively. It has both welcomed and deterred outsiders, receiving them with charm and politeness through its code of hospitality while using the same code to keep them at a distance. Before the war, it was the norm for government officials visiting the rural areas to be lavishly entertained and to be virtually imprisoned as guests in order to minimise the amount of information they could obtain for the purposes of taxation. Suspicions are rife and the rumour-mill is powerful.

The first mention of the area currently known as Afghanistan occurs in the Zoroastrian scriptures recorded during the reign of Cyrus the Great (d. 530 BC), who promoted Zoroastrianism throughout the Achaemenid empire. Darius the Great (550–486 BC) further extended the empire, which, at its height, reached from North Africa to the Indus river and included the full coastal area presently within Pakistan to the south of Afghanistan. Satrapies, or provinces, owing allegiance to the Achaemenid ruler were established in Herat, Balkh, Ghazni and along the Kabul river from Kabul to Peshawar. It is said that Darius faced constant difficulties subduing the small Afghan tribal kingdoms and had to maintain strong garrisons in the region (Dupree, 1980: 274). In spite of this, the Bactrians of Balkh fought with the Achaemenid forces when Alexander the Great (356–23 BC) overran the empire.

Alexander entered what is now Afghanistan in 330 BC, following the destruction of Persepolis and the murder of Darius the Third by three of his satraps. He built a city near Herat and continued to build new cities as he moved forward, in spite of fierce resistance from tribal leaders. His forward march took him south from Herat to Baluchistan and then east along the Helmand and Arghandab rivers towards Ghazni. From here he travelled northwards with his forces to the confluence of the Ghorband and Panjshir rivers, about 50 km north of what is now Kabul. In spite of the wintry conditions, his army crossed the Hindu Kush in the spring of 329 BC. It then quickly travelled north to the Oxus river (now called the Amu Darya), near present-day Kunduz, and attacked the resistance forces, forcing them out of their base at Balkh, which still exists to the west of Mazar-i-Sharif. Alexander's troops then crossed the Oxus and captured Marcanda (Samarkand).

Two years later, after a succession of hard-won military achievements in Central Asia, his remaining forces travelled south through Bamyan and the Ghorband Valley to the western reaches of modern-day Pakistan. Faced with rebellion, he was forced to abandon his expansionist ambitions and to lead his forces on a long retreat to Babylon, where he died in 323 BC leaving his empire to fragment among his Greek colonists, who remained in control, in one form or another, for a further two centuries.

The first and second centuries AD saw the development of the famous Silk Route between the Roman empire and China. Balkh was an important staging post on this route and there was a secondary route through Bamyan, Bagram and Jalalabad to India. China exported raw silk and India supplied cotton cloth, spices, ivory and semi-precious stones. Central Asia, including Afghanistan, exported rubies, lapis lazuli, silver and turquoise. The necessary stability was made possible by the Kushan dynasty, who originated as nomads in Central Asia and ruled from the lower Indus Valley to the Iranian frontier and from Chinese Sinkiang to the Caspian and Aral seas. However, this stability evaporated following the capture of the fragmenting Kushan empire by a Persian Zoroastrian dynasty known as the Sasanians, whose rule from AD 224 to AD 651 covered present-day Iraq, Iran, Afghanistan and southern Central Asia.

The Sasanian hold on the old Kushan empire was never strong and the various principalities into which it split were easily overrun by the Hephthalite Huns, who invaded from Central Asia in the latter part of the fifth century AD. The Hephthalite empire extended from Chinese Sinkiang to Iran and from Central Asia to the Punjab but it was equally unable to maintain a strong hold. It was, in turn, overrun by the Sasanians and western Turks in the middle of the sixth century. Their vassals lost power to the Arab invaders, who carried the message of Islam forward during the second quarter of the seventh century, reaching Kandahar in AD 699–700. However, the territory of Afghanistan again disintegrated, with the Kabul-based Hindu Shahi dynasty taking control of much of eastern Afghanistan, as vassals of the Ummayad Caliphs based in Damascus, until the ninth and tenth centuries AD.

A new force entered Afghanistan towards the end of the tenth century, made up of Turks from the north. These established the Ghaznavid dynasty, which ruled from AD 977 to 1186, conquering north-west India and the Punjab and capturing a large part of Iran, including Isfahan, in the process. The Ghaznavid period saw a significant level of conversion to Islam among the Hindu population of north-western India. The capital of the empire, Ghazni, was a centre of intellectual and artistic excellence. The empire went into a decline folowing the death of its major architect, Yamin Mahmud, in AD 1030.

However, it was Genghis Khan (1162–1227) who destroyed not only elements of this civilisation but many other civilisations in the wider region through a brutal wave of destruction, starting at his home in Mongolia and extending westwards to the Caspian. The area again fragmented after his ravages.

Unified control was achieved only under Tamerlane (1336–1405), a ruler of Turko-Mongol descent, whose empire stretched from Turkey to India. His successors patronised the arts and many ancient structures exist in Samarkand and Herat, including Herat's Friday Mosque, the shrine of Gowhar Shad and the minarets that stand at the entrance to the city. The Timurid period, as the reign of Tamerlane and his successors is known, lasted until 1506. Towards the end of the period, when Herat was the capital of the empire, poetry and miniaturism flourished.

Following the demise of the Timurid dynasty, Afghanistan was split between the Moghul and Safavid empires. The first Moghul ruler, Babar, was a descendant of both Tamerlane and Genghis Khan. Having been driven from the Fergana Valley in Central Asia by the Uzbeks, he moved south to take Kabul in 1504. From here he and his successors conquered most of India until this empire, which produced monuments such as the Taj Mahal, started to decline after the death of the last great Moghul emperor in 1707.

Simultaneously with the period of the Moghul empire, the Persian Safavid dynasty ruled Persia and western Afghanistan from 1501 to 1732. The two empires fought for control of Kandahar, which oscillated between them. They also had to contend with the Uzbeks from the north, who were driven from Herat by the Safavids and from Badakshan by the Moghuls. Finally, in 1648, the Moghuls gave up on their efforts to retain northern Afghanistan. They also faced revolts from the Pushtun tribes, which continued from 1658 to 1675. Similar revolts were encountered by the Safavids in Kandahar (1711) and Herat (1717).

In 1719 the new Afghan ruler of Kandahar, Mir Mahmoud, exploited the weakness of the Safavid empire by marching on the Persian cities of Kerman, Yazd and Isfahan, which by 1722 he had captured. His cousin Ashraf, who took power in 1725, defeated an Ottoman force in 1727 and was recognised by the Ottoman ruler as Shah of Persia. He nevertheless continued to recognise the Ottoman Sultan as titular head of the Muslim world.

However, the Safavids, under Nadir Shah, were able to recover control after inflicting a military defeat on Ashraf in 1729. During this brief expansionist phase, centred on Afghanistan, neither Mir Mahmoud nor Ashraf was able to exercise much control within Afghanistan beyond Kandahar, and what control they had was frequently threatened. The Safavids moved on Herat in 1732, Kandahar in 1738 and Lahore and Delhi in 1739. In return for generous gifts the Safavid ruler, Nadir Shah, allowed the Moghuls to retain control of Delhi and returned westwards to take Samarkand, Bukhara and Khiva in Central Asia, finally settling in Mashhad.

When Nadir Shah was assassinated a few years later, it was the turn of another Afghan leader, Ahmed Shah Durrani, to rise to prominence. Following his selection as leader of the Abdali tribe in 1747, he moved from Kandahar to take Ghazni, Kabul and Peshawar before making an attempt on Delhi. Meeting resistance from a stronger Moghul force, he had to retreat to Kandahar. In 1748 he tried again and a compromise was reached whereby the Moghul ruler ceded him territories west of the Indus river. Ahmed Shah then set his sights on Herat and Mashhad and, having achieved his objective, turned north-west to take over the Turkoman, Uzbek, Hazara and Tajik areas of what is presently northern Afghanistan. He then took Kashmir.

Towards the end of his life, Ahmed Shah faced increasing problems as he struggled to retain his dominions. Following insurrections by the Sikhs in the Punjab, he finally lost control of this area in 1767. In the north, he encountered threats to the captured provinces from the Amir of Bukhara, and these were withdrawn only when the two sides agreed to accept the Amu Darya as the boundary between their spheres of control. As a symbol of their agreement the Amir presented Ahmed Shah with a cloak said to have been worn by the Prophet Muhammad, and Ahmed Shah had a mosque constructed in Kandahar to house the garment. Two centuries later this cloak was held up before an assembled crowd by the Taliban leader, Mullah Omar, in Kandahar.

Ahmed Shah died in 1772 and his son and successor, Timur Shah, moved the capital to Kabul, following growing tensions with the local Pushtun in Kandahar. Over the following five years he lost control of

Kashmir and Sind in the east, Balkh in the north and Khurasan and Sistan in the west. He also faced a new Uzbek force from the north after 1784 in the form of the Bukhara-based Mangit dynasty, which ruled until 1921.

Timur Shah's death in 1793 heralded a prolonged period of disunity, which saw growing competition between the Russian and British empires as each sought to stop the other gaining a hold over the area, including the various khanates of Central Asia. A constant stream of Russian and British intelligence officers roamed the region seeking to build alliances and to explore the various routes advancing armies could take. An early success on the part of the British was a treaty of mutual defence against Russia and France, signed in 1809 between Shah Shuja, the son of Timur Shah, and a British delegation.

In 1837 the British governor-general, Lord Auckland, sent a delegation to the then ruler in Kabul, Dost Muhammad, to encourage him to make peace with the Sikh ruler, Ranjit Singh (who had, in 1819, seized Peshawar, northern Punjab and Kashmir, resulting in an inconclusive resort to arms by Dost Muhammad against the Sikhs), and to renew the mutual security agreement signed in 1809. However, as the British delegation continued its discussions in Kabul a Persian army, aided by seconded Russian officers, laid siege to Herat. Russia also sent a delegate to hold discussions with Dost Muhammad. Although the Afghan ruler failed to conclude an agreement with either Britain or Russia and the siege of Herat failed, the Russian presence had alarmed hawks within the British Indian government, who decided that Britain had to make absolutely sure that Afghanistan was not vulnerable to Russian influence or invasion.

In 1838, Lord Auckland announced that an invasion force would be sent into Afghan territory to restore to power Shah Shuja, who had been ousted soon after signing the 1809 mutual defence treaty. The following year, the combined British and Indian troops entered Afghanistan from the south and took Kandahar, Ghazni and Kabul. Assuming that their occupation was well established they proceeded to import their wives and children and the colonial lifestyle they had developed in India, but it took only two years for popular resentment to manifest itself in armed insurrection. As the situation rapidly deteriorated, the British agreed to sign a treaty that provided for the restoration of Dost Muhammad as ruler in Kabul. However, they failed to wait while a promised Afghan escort was organised to lead them safely out of Afghanistan. The retreating men, women and children were harassed as they moved forward through the thick January snow and they died in their thousands, either from their wounds or from exposure. Only one person made it to Jalalabad to recount what had happened. A few others survived after being taken prisoner. The following August the British sent a revenge force to Kabul, inflicting further casualties and destroying the ancient Kabul bazaar. They then withdrew.

Following the British departure, Dost Muhammad captured Mazar-i-Sharif, Kunduz, Badakshan and Kandahar and, for a period, occupied Peshawar. In May 1863, one month before he died, he added Herat to his domain. He was succeeded by his son, Sher Ali Khan, who ruled, with a short gap, until 1879, but not without serious attempts by his brothers to unseat him.

Over this period Russia, concerned at Britain's intervention in Afghanistan, proceeded to annex the Central Asian khanates or to bring them under its sphere of influence. When, in 1869, the Amir of Bukhara submitted to vassal status, Russia was effectively sitting on the northern bank of the Amu Darya river. Under the Anglo-Russian Agreement of 1872, Britain and Russia tacitly agreed to the Amu Darya as the northern frontier of Afghanistan. In 1873, under pressure from Britain, Russia agreed to the creation of a corridor of land to divide Russia from British India in north-eastern Afghanistan. The Wakhan of Badakshan thus brought Afghanistan face to face with China amidst the Himalayan heights.

The Afghan ruler, Sher Ali, became increasingly anxious at the steady Russian military advance into Central Asia and sought assurances from Britain that it would provide support if the northern border was transgressed. However, he refused requests by Britain to have a European-manned mission in Kabul, arguing that Russia would demand the same. As Russia advanced on the Central Asian principalities of Khiva and Merv in 1878, in response to the British military occupation of Quetta in 1876 and military setbacks in the Dardanelles of Turkey at the hands of the British, it dispatched a Russian mission to Kabul in spite of Sher Ali's remonstrations. The British demanded that they also be permitted to station a mission in Kabul. Sher Ali, who was in mourning for his son, was slow to respond. A British mission was nevertheless sent but, when it was refused onward progress to Kabul, Britain responded by sending an invasion force to Afghanistan.

Sher Ali travelled to the north bank of the Amu Darya and sought permission to travel to St Petersburg to request support from the Tsar. He was rebuffed, and died in Balkh in February 1879 before he could set out for Kabul. His son and successor, Yaqub Khan, was not in a strong position to stand up to the British demands and in May 1879 reluctantly signed the Treaty of Gandamak, which provided that Britain would control Afghanistan's foreign affairs and that British-born representatives would be permitted to be stationed in Kabul.

The first representative arrived in July 1879 and was assassinated the following September. British forces then marched into Kabul, prompting the Amir to abdicate. The British commander, General Roberts, became the effective ruler in Kabul until July 1880, when Abdur-Rahman Khan, a nephew of Sher Ali, who had lived in exile for twelve years in Samarkand and Tashkent, crossed the Amu Darya and gathered a following in northern Afghanistan, sufficient to allow him to proclaim himself Amir of Afghanistan.

The British accepted his claim and withdrew from Kabul in August 1880, prompted by the defeat, towards the end of July, of a British force at Maiwand near Kandahar. General Roberts in Kabul gathered a large army and marched on Kandahar to reverse the defeat. In spite of its success, the British did not remain. A new Liberal government, which had come to power in Britain under Gladstone in April 1880 and was less enthusiastic than its predecessor over British involvement in Afghanistan, had decided that British forces should withdraw from the country.

The British government did, however, provide military and financial support to Abdur-Rahman, who from the very beginning faced internal opposition to his rule. With his control not extending much beyond Kabul, he set out to conquer all the territory that lay between the Russian, British and Persian spheres of influence. This he achieved by 1896, penetrating even into remote areas such as the Hazarajat. He also dealt with opponents among the Pushtun tribes in the south by forcibly relocating them to the area north of the Hindu Kush. There they represented, and continue to represent, a Pushtun element in the midst of the Turkoman, Uzbek, Hazara and Tajik populations, a factor that has provided a foothold for the Taliban in the north.

In spite of his links with the British government, Abdur-Rahman was careful not to upset the religious establishment of the Ulema (men of religious learning who interpret Shari'a law) and mullahs (traditional prayer leaders) by allowing Western influences to creep into the country. He nevertheless ensured that they were not able to exercise a significant level of power within the government.

The continuing tensions between Russia and Britain finally resulted in agreements being drawn up in 1891 and 1895–96 to fix the present northern frontiers of Afghanistan. The Durand line, agreed in 1893, delineated the boundary between Afghanistan and British India, effectively cutting the Pushtun population in half.

Abdur-Rahman died in 1901 and was succeeded by his eldest son, Habibullah. While Abdur-Rahman had exercised a high degree of control over the religious leaders, Habibullah allowed them to exercise power at the level of the state and to have a significant influence on policy. At the same time he allowed the beginnings of a reform movement to emerge, manifested in the publication by Mahmud Tarzi of the bi-monthly newspaper *Seraj Al-Akbar*. This attacked both European imperialism and the resistance to change by the religious leadership, challenging the assumption that the Muslim world had nothing to learn from the West. Habibullah was particularly noteworthy for his success in keeping both Britain and Russia at bay and in fiercely maintaining Afghanistan's independence and neutrality, even during the First World War. He was assassinated in 1919 and replaced by his son, Amanullah.

Within months of taking power Amanullah declared war on Britain, seeking to exploit reports of its post-war weakness. Although it was successful in reversing an initial defeat, Britain had no taste for further fighting and agreed, through the 1919 Treaty of Rawalpindi, that Afghanistan was free to conduct its own foreign affairs. Immediately after the signing of the Treaty of Rawalpindi, the newly formed Afghan government established contact with the Soviet Union through an exchange of missions, and a Treaty of Friendship was signed in May 1921. Missions were also sent to Europe and the USA to establish diplomatic relations. Thus ended Britain's attempts to exercise control. The failure of the British to colonise Afghanistan remains an important source of pride amongst Afghans in the invincibility of their country.

The Anglo-Afghan Treaty, also signed in 1921, failed to resolve the thorny question of jurisdiction over the Pushtun tribes on the British Indian side of the Durand line. Afghanistan sought a loose suzerainty over these but Britain refused, out of fear that the Pushtuns could foment unrest in British India and further upset the increasingly fragile hold of the British in the Indian subcontinent.

The Soviet Union was also facing unrest in Central Asia, where the rebels were receiving support from volunteers from Afghanistan and India. In spite of this Amanullah received military aircraft from the Soviet Union, together with assistance to develop telephone links between the main cities.

Internally, Amanullah had to deal with armed revolts by the Pushtun tribes against the reform and modernisation programmes he had set in motion. He was concerned at what he saw as the backwardness of Afghanistan relative to the West and felt that the only way to strengthen it, on the religious and cultural levels, was to modernise it. He undertook a seven-month tour of Europe in 1928, fuelling rumours that he was turning against Islam. When, on his return, he attempted to impose Western dress codes and co-education, the opposition intensified. Having ignored advice that he should build up his army before introducing a reform programme, Amanullah was unable to resist the armed onslaught of the rebels and fled into exile.

Amanullah was overthrown by a Tajik, Habibullah II, who led the rebel advance. Habibullah II was ousted nine months later by a Pushtun, Muhammad Nadir Khan, a former commander of Amanullah's army, who had been highly critical of Amanullah's attempts to introduce radical changes into Afghanistan. He was not only concerned that the king had not taken sufficient account of the need to back his reform programme with a reasonably strong army; he was also convinced that any programme of reform had to be tackled with extreme caution in the face of the ultra-conservatism of rural society. In September 1930 a council of tribal and religious leaders, or Loya Jirga, convened by Nadir Khan, accorded him the title of king and decreed that the Hanafi Shari'a law of Sunni Islam should be the prevailing legal code. However, the 1931 Constitution created confusion by providing for religious and secular legal systems to operate in parallel. The more severe punishments prescribed under Shari'a law, such as amputation for theft, nevertheless became increasingly rare as the years progressed.

Nadir Khan was assassinated in 1933 and was succeeded by his 19-year-old son, Zahir Shah, who, although he reigned for 40 years, was subject to the guidance of his uncles for much of his rule. Afghanistan remained neutral during the Second World War, in spite of strong relations with Germany, Italy and Japan during the preceding years.

The immediate post-war period saw early negotiations for the independence of India, based on partition between India and Pakistan. The Afghan government took the opportunity provided by the negotiations to argue that the Pushtun tribal areas of North-West Frontier Province, which had held a semi-independent status in relation to British India since 1901, should be able to opt for independence. In spite of these arguments, Pakistan was born in 1947 with the tribal areas incorporated. However, it was not long before Pakistan had to resort to arms against tribal uprisings and, in 1949, a Pakistan air force strike on the tribal area led to a village on the Afghan side of the border being bombed. The Afghan government responded by reneging on all the treaties that had determined the frontier of Afghanistan with British India and supported an initiative to create a 'Pushtunistan' assembly on the Pakistan side of the Durand line. In return, Pakistan imposed a blockade on petroleum products travelling to Afghanistan. The Kabul government promptly signed a barter agreement with the Soviet Union in July 1950 whereby the latter would provide petroleum products and other important commodities in return for Afghan wool and raw cotton. The Soviet Union also agreed to allow free transit for Afghan goods through its territory, and commenced oil exploration in northern Afghanistan.

Afghanistan thus increasingly looked to the Soviet Union as a trading partner and source of support. A $100m loan followed in 1955 and the first major consignment of arms arrived a year later, after several failed attempts on the part of the Afghan government to obtain arms from the USA. The Soviet Union also assisted in the further development of military airfields near Mazar-i-Sharif in the north, Shindand in the west and Bagram, north of Kabul. The USA was involved on a much smaller scale, commencing with two major dam projects in the Helmand basin, together with a major highway that linked up with another built by the Soviet Union to bring the urban centres of Afghanistan within easy travelling distance of each other for the first time.

The process of *rapprochement* with the USSR and the USA was accelerated during the period in office of Muhammad Daoud Khan, who served as prime minister from 1953 to 1963. He also restarted the process of reform that had been moribund since the fall of Amanullah in 1929. In August 1959, Daoud and senior members of the government appeared on a public platform with their wives and daughters unveiled. The inevitable protests by the religious leadership were put down by the army, strengthened with Soviet assistance, and a gradual process commenced of women entering the urban workforce. When the army was used in Kandahar to enforce tax collection, rioters targeted a girls' school, a women's public bath and a cinema as symbols of the opposed modernisation.

Afghanistan was pushed even further into the hold of the Soviet Union when diplomatic relations between Pakistan and Afghanistan were cut in 1961 over the Pushtunistan issue, resulting in the closure of the border and a halt to transit trade through Pakistan. The border remained closed until 1963, when Daoud's resignation made a compromise with Pakistan possible.

Immediately following Daoud's resignation, King Zahir Shah gave added impetus to the process of constitutional reform started by Daoud. A Constitutional Advisory Committtee, which included two women, was set up. Among the more important provisions of the 1964 Constitution was the legal equality of both women and men. The Constitution also gave precedence to the secular legal system over Shari'a law, thus overturning the 1931 Constitution. It nevertheless stated that 'Islam is the sacred religion of Afghanistan' and provided that Hanafi Shari'a law should be the last resort where no existing secular law applied. In addition, it stipulated that an elected parliament be set up, together with 28 provincial councils. A proportion of the individuals to be included in the parliament were to be women, some nominated by the king. The first parliament, elected in 1965, had four women MPs out of a total of 216.

The late 1960s witnessed growing dissent as young people came to the capital from other parts of the country to take advantage of expanded education opportunities, particularly in Kabul University, and found a system that was still highly elitist. Radical movements found fertile ground amongst Kabul's student population. Some advocated a much faster process of reform and found a vehicle in the People's Democratic Party of Afghanistan (PDPA). Others vociferously opposed the changes that had already taken place and fought for a return to Islamic values.

The Islamist parties, as they were called, set out to establish a political movement that would work for the creation of an Islamic state based on Shari'a law. Among the ready recruits were the sons of Tajiks and Uzbeks who had fled to northern Afghanistan from the religious persecution perpetrated by the Soviet government across Central Asia during the 1920s and 1930s.

The following years were ones of considerable unrest, with the socialist and Islamist parties growing in strength. A disastrous three-year famine from 1969 to 1972 tested the government's effectiveness and integrity to its limits and it was found wanting. Finally, Zahir Shah was deposed in July 1973 by his cousin and former prime minister, Daoud.

Daoud looked to the army and to the moderate wing of the split PDPA to provide his power base. Several members of the PDPA became members of Daoud's Central Committee. Daoud embarked on a process of further reform, including land reform, but was mindful of the need to proceed cautiously in order to avoid a backlash from conservative rural opinion. Tensions quickly developed and PDPA members were removed from the government. Daoud then went on the offensive against all potential opponents, forcing the Islamist parties to flee to Pakistan. At the same time he sought to reduce his dependence on the Soviet Union through increasing overtures to the West and strengthened links with Iran.

On 17 April 1978 Daoud was overthrown and killed in a military coup orchestrated by the PDPA, with possible Soviet backing. The extreme radicalism of the new government and its purges of opponents prompted large numbers of professionals to leave for Pakistan, Europe and the USA. In the countryside, ignoring the reactions to Amanullah's earlier attempts to introduce rapid reforms, the PDPA immediately took measures to create a ceiling on landholdings, reduce rural indebtedness, limit the brideprice and set a minimum age for marriage. A mass literacy campaign was also embarked upon as part of a secular education programme aimed at girls and boys, women and men, young and old.

As with Amanullah, no attempt was made to build a gradual process of reform from below. The measures ignored the complexities of land tenure and rural relationships, and the literacy programme was implemented without regard for the requirement that women and girls be educated separately. Offence was taken at the use of male teachers from the cities to instruct women and girls and at the educational material, which seemed to relate to a socialist Utopia rather than to the realities of rural Afghanistan. Old people felt humiliated at being forcibly taught by people a fraction of their own age.

The PDPA's use of force in bringing the changes to fruition, combined with a brutal disregard for societal and religious sensitivities, resulted in a massive backlash from the rural population, including those elements in whose interests the PDPA felt it was acting. The anger of the population found an appropriate outlet in the unifying call for a jihad. One area after another exploded in violence against the regime, and government forces were called upon to respond with even greater violence. Large-scale desertions from the army followed.

Interestingly, it was the non-tribal areas of the north, including the Shi'a zone of central Afghanistan, that launched the first insurrections. The Pushtun tribes were more ready to believe well of the PDPA government by virtue of its predominantly Pushtun membership. It was only when the Soviet Union invaded that the tribes joined the resistance *en masse*. Furthermore, the Islamists, who originated in the north, had no illusions about the objectives of the PDPA, having rubbed shoulders with them in Kabul University. Jamiat (p. 30), in particular, had the necessary combination of organisational strengths and respect for tradition to enable them to build mass support. The early resistance was therefore, to a degree, a rising up of the element within Afghan society that had been marginalised by the ruling Pushtun establishment, with its tribal foundations. It was also a manifestation of educated youth taking power from the old aristocracy, building a new alliance with the Ulema and developing links with tribal leaders outside the aristocracy. The new resistance leadership encouraged a return to Shari'a law as the primary legal code.

The Soviet Union had taken advantage of the PDPA's assumption of power by engaging ever more deeply in Afghanistan on the economic, political and military fronts. In December 1978, an agreement was signed empowering the Kabul government to call on Moscow for direct military assistance if the need arose. The Kremlin was far from happy at the way the situation was unfolding in Afghanistan, but felt it had no choice but to back the PDPA. With the overthrow of the Shah of Iran by an Islamist government, Moscow was nervous at the possibility that the Islamists in Afghanistan might exploit any ambivalence it might manifest towards the PDPA regime. Internal power struggles within the PDPA leadership led to the overthrow and subsequent assassination of President Nur Muhammad Taraki in September 1979 and his replacement by President Hafizullah Amin. However, Amin demonstrated an independence from Moscow's bidding that made the Soviets anxious for their future interests in Afghanistan.

There has been much speculation as to why the Soviet Union invaded Afghanistan towards the end of December 1979, but the evidence suggests that Moscow's historical fear of encirclement from the south was the dominant factor. Indications that the USA might strengthen the Islamic resistance, and fears that it might have ambitions to establish a military presence there if conditions allowed, combined with a growing *rapprochement* between Washington and Peking to create an acute sense of paranoia in the Kremlin. The Soviet invasion resulted in the death of President Amin. He was replaced by a relatively moderate member of the PDPA, Babrak Karmal, who arrived from Moscow shortly after the invasion.

Soviet forces remained in Afghanistan until 15 February 1989. Their decision to withdraw, taken in 1986 and given written form in the Geneva Accords of 14 April 1988, was as much a consequence of internal factors within the Soviet Union as of military defeat. The Soviet economy was showing serious signs of strain and could ill afford a major overseas war. Furthermore, veterans from the war were returning angry and disillusioned and made their feelings known through a wave of protests. Internal changes in the Politburo were also influential. Mikhail Gorbachov, who came to power in 1985, did not share the bellicose tendencies of his predecessors and was able gradually to build up a body of support for an ending to Soviet military involvement. In the end, the processes that had led to the decision to withdraw also resulted in the collapse of the Soviet Union itself in 1991, heralding the emergence of a Mujahidin government in April 1992.

3 The Mujahidin

The point of departure for the Islamists is not the everyday experience of Islam, that is to say Islam interpreted as a cultural form, but a political insight. For many of them, their return to religion has been brought about through their experience in politics and not as a result of their religious belief. The Ulema define politics on the basis of relations within society as established by law; the state is the means by which justice is able to operate within Moslem society. It is the Moslems, or rather the community of Moslems, who provide the basis for political thought; politics is an extension of law. For Islamists, the nature of society is predetermined by the nature of the state (Roy, 1986: 80).

This analysis is of interest in that it clearly encapsulates the basic division between two elements of what has come to be known as the Mujahidin movement. It also indicates a complexity in a picture that has, through repetitive media images of Afghan warriors launching rockets and shells from mountain tops, been presented in a highly simplistic manner.

A key element in a consideration of the Mujahidin movement is the extent to which the parties that were seen to represent it were in fact representative. To take this forward, one needs to be clear about definitions. At the very least, one can say that all the Afghans who took up arms against the PDPA and the Soviet forces, who regarded themselves as engaged in a jihad, were, in the true sense, Mujahidin, or fighters in a holy war. The fighters found their own leaders at the local level and some of these rose to prominence. The resistance movement also benefited from mass desertions from the PDPA army, forcing Soviet soldiers, who had hoped to leave this to the Afghan forces, to engage in direct combat.

The jihad legitimised, in religious terms, the large-scale exodus of a significant proportion of the population to neighbouring Islamic countries, in that Afghanistan had been transgressed by a secular force and therefore ceased to be Islamic. The flight of Muhammad from Mecca to Medina in AD 622, in the face of harassment and physical attacks, provides the necessary precedent for this religious right. A total of 3.2 million refugees made their way to Pakistan, where they were accommodated in camps the length of the border, primarily in North-West Frontier Province but also in Baluchistan and Punjab. In the camps, they were provided with food rations and had access to health and education facilities. A similar number, 2.9 million, went to Iran. Here they were largely integrated into the economy and had access to health and education services on the same basis as poor Iranians; they also benefited from entitlements to subsidies on basic essentials. A proportion were settled in camps along the border, from which they were given support by the Iranian government to cross the border into Afghanistan to fight against the Soviet forces (BAAG, 1997).

The definition of Mujahidin thus encompasses all those who moved to Pakistan and Iran, and engaged in fighting within Afghanistan on the basis of incursionary movements from these two countries, together with the many people who opted to remain in Afghanistan throughout the war, often fleeing to the sanctuary of the mountains with their families and organising raids from there. Some of these were affiliated to organised groups. Others acted spontaneously as part of their village or tribal communities. Yet others, primarily Tajiks, fled to to the cities, causing them to swell in size. Kabul thus has a significant Tajik, Persian-speaking, population.

The leaders of the Islamist parties, who had fled to Pakistan in the mid-1970s, saw the opportunity provided by the declaration of a jihad to claim leadership over the resistance movement. The purges of their members by the Daoud government had left them in a much weakened state and they were open to overtures by the Pakistani government aimed at securing particular objectives geared to Pakistan's interests if, in return, they were given support.

When the leaders first arrived in Pakistan they were welcomed by the then president, Zulfikar Bhutto. He is said to have seen them as potentially strengthening his hand in relation to the highly sensitive issue of Pushtunistan, on which President Daoud of Afghanistan took an aggressive line (Arney, 1990: 132). Bhutto permitted the parties to establish offices in Peshawar and also provided them with the where-withal to organise armed insurrections within Afghanistan, hoping that these would have a destabilising effect on Daoud's regime. However, the arrests and executions that resulted from the failure of most of these attempted uprisings further weakened the Islamist movement.

Following the hanging of Bhutto by the new president of Pakistan, Zia Al-Haq, the Islamist parties found a leader whose ideological aspirations for Pakistan were very much in line with their own thinking and with the thinking of similar parties in Pakistan, such as the Jamaat-i-Islami. Zia had a clear ambition to establish in Kabul a government over which Pakistan could exercise control. The strategy behind this was one that was central to Pakistan's defence: to create strategic strength against India through the formation of an Islamic bloc stretching from Pakistan to Central Asia. Zia was, however, wary of the Pushtun tribes, whose tradition of fierce independence made them unlikely partners in a defensive coalition. He therefore looked for allies amongst Afghans who had an ideological basis for their resistance to the Soviet Union, and the Islamists seemed suitable candidates. However, he was reluctant to give too much support too quickly. There were inevitable dangers in unleashing a powerful and uncoordinated movement before it could be brought under control.

The decision of the USA to provide first covert aid, in 1979, and then overt aid on a massive scale from 1986 onwards, using Pakistan as a conduit, made it possible for the Islamist parties to move from a position of weakness to one in which they served as a major channel for arms and other resources to the Mujahidin fighting within Afghanistan. However, there was considerable resistance to this assumed leadership role from the spontaneous leadership that had emerged within Afghanistan. Numerous new organisations sprang up and petitioned the Pakistan government for military supplies. The government responded at the end of 1980 by stating that it would recognise only seven of the many parties or groups in existence, and that all those seeking military hard-ware would have to affiliate themselves with one or other of these. Four of these so-called Mujahidin parties were Islamist, in that they sought to create a political movement with an ideological basis that drew on a reinterpretation of the essential elements of Islam. The other three are normally referred to as traditionalists, in that they emerged from traditional tribal or other groupings within Afghanistan.

The parties, with their leadership, were as follows.

Jamiat-i-Islami, formed in 1972 out of an informal grouping that had emerged during the 1960s, was the first of the Islamist parties to be established in Kabul. Its leader, Burhannudin Rabbani, was a lecturer in Islamic theology at Kabul University. He was much influenced by the Muslim Brotherhood movement in Egypt and by its ability to create a mass following. The party set out to achieve a radical restructuring of all aspects of society to accord with a particular interpretation of Islamic principles, and thus aimed to incorporate the political, economic, judicial, social and economic systems within the Islamic sphere. However, Rabbani took the view that, in seeking to promote an Islamist direction, the party should proceed cautiously and with respect for existing beliefs, traditions and practices, including the traditional emphasis on consensual decision-making. He is therefore very much a moderate and a pragmatist, and his academic origins and solid learning have been important influences on him. Differences within Jamiat-i-Islami as to the tactics to be adopted in furthering the objectives of the party led to a split in 1976 and to the emergence of new parties. Rabbani felt strongly that a broad popular movement should be built up before attempts were made to seek power. Others favoured more radical options. Rabbani fled to Pakistan to avoid arrest by President Daoud. As an ethnic Tajik, Rabbani has been identified geographically with north-eastern Afghanistan.

Another key member of Jamiat-i-Islami was Ahmed Shah Masoud, who joined while an engineering student at Kabul University. He played a major role during the period of Soviet occupation in leading the resistance forces in the Panjshir Valley, to the north-east of Kabul. He also created a civilian administration in the area, which lacked governmental structures. Following the capture of Kabul in April 1992, he took responsibility for the defence and policing of the capital. Masoud played a major leadership role in resisting the Taliban advance from 1996 to 2001. He was assassinated in September 2001. Like Rabbani, he was a Tajik.

Hisb-e-Islami (Hekmatyar) arose out of a split, in 1979, within Hisb-e-Islami, which had come into being because of the split within Jamiat-i-Islami. Its leader, Gulbuddin Hekmatyar, an engineering student at Kabul University during the formative years of the Islamist movement, is from Kunduz in northern Afghanistan. He is an ethnic Pushtun, possibly descended from the Pushtuns relocated to northern Afghanistan at the end of the last century by Abdur-Rahman. In Hisb-e-Islami he adopted the Soviet organisational model, creating a movement based on a cell structure with a pyramidal chain of authority. Potential members were carefully vetted and had to undergo a probationary period. Hekmatyar is much more of a purist than Rabbani and sought to eradicate existing customs, practices and structures and to replace them with a new, highly organised structure geared specifically to the creation of an Islamic state. Hekmatyar never had much of a geographical base within Afghanistan and relied heavily on the refugee camps, on Nangarhar Province in eastern Afghanistan, and on Kunduz as recruiting grounds. Hisb-e-Islami (Hekmatyar) tended to appeal to relatively well-educated young radicals, many of whom have benefited from a technical education. It regarded education as an important means of transmitting its ideology and operated a number of schools in Pakistan, including schools for girls. Hekmatyar has been virtually powerless since the Taliban capture of Kabul in 1996 and has been living in exile in Iran for the past few years.

Hisb-e-Islami (Khalis) emerged as a splinter movement from Hisb-e-Islami in 1979 after Younis Khalis, a tribal leader from Paktia Province with radical Islamic leanings, opted to pursue his own directions. Khalis was trained in Islamic theology at the Deoband School in Delhi, which produced several generations of Afghan Ulema. His attacks in the press on Daoud's reforms meant that he had to flee to Pakistan. His style of leadership is that of the tribal patriarch, and his following has been largely based on traditional religious leaders and local commanders in south-eastern Afghanistan. Mullah Omar is said to have aligned himself to Hisb-e-Islami (Khalis) during the period of resistance to the Soviet occupation.

Ittihad-i-Islami was formed by Abdul Rasoul Sayyaf, a former theology lecturer from Kabul University and a fluent Arabic speaker, who served as Rabbani's deputy in the early Islamist movement within the university. Imprisoned for his activities by the PDPA regime of 1978–79, he was released as part of the amnesty that followed the Soviet invasion and fled to Pakistan, where he established his own Islamist party. Ittihad-i-Islami has never had a significant geographical base outside Kabul and has always been strongly associated with Saudi Arabia, which has provided much of the backing. However, in spite of many similarities between its ideology and that of the Saudi Wahabbis, the party insists that it is distinct from that movement, which has established a particularly strong presence in Kunar in north-eastern Afghanistan. It has, however, demonstrated strong opposition to the Shi'a minority in Afghanistan, echoing Riyadh's competition with Tehran for pre-eminence within the Islamic world. Sayyaf has been part of the opposition alliance operating in the north-east since 1996.

The *Afghan National Liberation Front* was established by Sibghatullah Mujadidi in 1980, and is one of the three parties referred to as traditionalist by virtue of its absence of ideology and of its power base within the rural society of Afghanistan. Mujadidi comes from an important Pushtun family, which heads one of the branches of the Sufi Naqshbandi order in southern Afghanistan and has links with the former ruling establishment. Although he comes from a conservative tradition and has been a strong advocate for the return of King Zahir Shah, he was active in radical Islamic circles during the 1950s and 1960s, establishing contact with the Muslim Brotherhood in Egypt, and was jailed for four and a half years by Daoud in 1959 for campaigning against a visit by Khrushchev. The ANLF was never able to attract a good share of the military resources earmarked for the Mujahidin.

Harakat-i-Inqilab-i-Islami emerged in 1980, under the leadership of Nabi Muhammadi, an Islamic scholar. The party's power base lies amongst the Ulema and village mullahs who led the early revolts against the PDPA, together with the students, or *talibs*, of the *madrasah* (Islamic schools) at which the Ulema taught. It attracted an enormous following during the first year because of what it represented, but it did not have the organisational capacity to provide adequately for the needs of its adherents and many gravitated to Jamiat or Hisb-e-Islami (Khalis), which were regarded as sufficiently moderate and respectful of tradition to justify their allegiance. Of the parties, it is the closest in its beliefs to the creed of the Taliban. It saw itself as having no ideology and sought a return to the strict application of Islamic law and to the primacy of the Shari'a, without espousing an Islamist direction. It also constituted an organised movement, with Ulema and *talibs* establishing what were termed fronts, centred on local *madrasahs*. However, the party head-quarters was not able to support this network effectively.

Mahaz-i-Milli-i-Islami is headed by Pir Gailani, a religious leader con-nected with the Sufi movement and with an inherited spiritual status, who has a strong following among the Pushtun tribes of southern Afghanistan. His connection by marriage to the royal family and his close links with the former ruling Durrani establishment have made him a consistent supporter of the former king, Zahir Shah, a position held by much of the population of Kandahar. The party is therefore the effective mouthpiece of the former establishment. Pir Gailani is a moderate and a liberal and has thus represented the views of what was left of the educated professional classes to a greater extent than the other Mujahidin leaders.

From the time that these parties were designated as channels for military aid, it became difficult to determine to what extent the various groups inside Afghanistan were affiliating themselves to one party or another because of the resources on offer, and to what extent conviction was the deciding factor. The fact that, within any given village or family, more than one party might be represented added to the confusion. However, it is possible to identify particular geographical areas as having been predominantly linked to particular parties.

Thus Jamiat had a strong following in the Shomali Valley north of Kabul and in Kapisa, Takhar and Badakshan, all in the north-east. It was also represented through Ismail Khan in north-western Afghanistan. Hekmatyar's Hisb-e-Islami was able to generate a scattered following in the provinces of Nangarhar and Kunduz, together with the city of Baghlan, to the south of Kunduz. Younis Khalis had his base in Paktia. Gailani had strong support in Kandahar. Mujadidi and Muhammadi were represented in pockets throughout the south.

It proved difficult for Jamiat to build up its movement in the Pushtun

tribal areas and it always remained a party that represented the northern minorities, particularly the Tajiks. This was, in large part, due to
the fact that the de-tribalised society of the north did not have the
structures to withstand the influence of a well-organised movement.
The tribal leaders in the south, in contrast, were resistant to any influences from outside.

The Pakistani government, perhaps in the hope of maintaining a
degree of control over the refugee population, encouraged the Mujahidin
parties to set up offices in many of the refugee camps and also to establish
their own camps. Refugees had to become members of whichever party
held sway in their particular camps in order to claim rations. The parties
recruited within the camps for men and teenagers to fight for them and
the camps became bases for incursionary attacks into Afghanistan, with
the result that the parties became enormously powerful.

Of the parties, the Hisb-e-Islami party of Gulbuddin Hekmatyar
found particular favour with those elements within Pakistan that were
providing support to the Mujahidin, notably the Jamaat-e-Islami Party
and the Inter-Services Intelligence (Arney, 1990). The USA was assumed
to be aware of this imbalance but was said to have condoned it on the
basis of Hisb-e-Islami's apparently greater organisational capacity.

The seven parties, which formed themselves into the Seven Party
Alliance in May 1985, were all adherents of Sunni Islam and all but
one, Jamiat, were Pushtun. In addition, there were two Shi'a parties.
The larger of the two, Hisb-e-Wahdat, was formed with the encourage-
ment of the Iranian government to bring the various Afghan parties
based in Iran under one umbrella and so strengthen the bargaining
power of the Shi'as in the internal struggle for power within Afghanistan. Hisb-e-Wahdat took control of the Hazarajat area of central
Afghanistan in 1987, under the leadership of Abdul Ali Mazari. The
other Shi'a party, another Harakat-i-Islami, is led by Sheikh Assef
Muhsini, whose following has been among urban educated Shi'as. Muhsini has often played a role as a mediator as the major players have
fought for dominance.

The war between the Soviet forces and the Mujahidin went through
several phases. From 1979 to 1986, when Babrak Karmal was president
of the Soviet-backed government, the combined government and
Soviet forces were very much on the offensive. This was consistent

with the hawkish policies of Leonid Brezhnev, Yuri Andropov and Konstantin Chernenko. When Mikhail Gorbachov took over the Kremlin in 1985, after an initial period of energetically pursuing the military option, he started a shift in policy that finally led to a decision to withdraw from Afghanistan. His arrival coincided with a decision by President Ronald Reagan in 1985 to increase substantially US support to the Mujahidin. This included supplying them with Stinger missiles, which enabled the Mujahidin to shoot down the helicopters and low-flying aircraft that had inflicted great damage and loss of life on the countryside. There are many who claim that the Stingers were instrumental in turning the tide of the war against the Russians. That is quite possible, but it is also important to recognise that Gorbachov may have decided to close the Afghan chapter because of the serious problems he was facing at home.

From 1987, the Soviet Union demonstrated an increasing commitment to the UN-sponsored peace negotiations that had been going on throughout the war, involving Pakistan, the USA and the Afghan government, but excluding the Mujahidin parties. The consequent signing in April 1988 of the Geneva Accords, which envisaged that Soviet troops would withdraw from Afghanistan on 15 February 1989, made no provision for a new government of Afghanistan, assuming a continuation of the Soviet-backed one, and therefore disregarded the Mujahidin parties as potential participants in a future administration. The Soviet government had, however, taken steps to make the PDPA government more acceptable to the population. These included replacing Babrak Karmal with Muhammad Najibullah in 1986, in order to present a less doctrinaire face. President Najibullah proved himself to be extremely adept at buying the support of the traditional leaders throughout the country – a policy previously adopted by his predecessor, but with less success.

The international community nevertheless anticipated that the Soviet-backed government of President Najibullah would fall immediately after the Soviet withdrawal. In anticipation of this, Pakistan and the USA put strong pressure on the Seven Party Alliance to form a government-in-waiting. Under the glare of the world's TV cameras, the Mujahidin leaders held lengthy meetings during the last days of the Soviet occupation. Agreement between them proved to be elusive, but the Seven Party

Alliance was re-formed into the Afghan Interim Government only days before the withdrawal.

At the same time, the UN launched a high-profile appeal for international assistance to support the anticipated repatriation of the six million refugees in Pakistan and Iran, assuming, not unreasonably, that the departure of the Soviet-backed government would signal an end to the jihad. In the event, 15 February came and went and, although the Soviet troops left as promised, the Najibullah government showed no signs of collapse. The Afghan Interim Government set out to create legitimacy for itself by establishing an alternative capital within Afghanistan. Jalalabad was chosen as the most suitable base and the Mujahidin proceeded to besiege the city, using an enormous quantity of firepower. However, they failed in their attempt and it took another three years before the Soviet-backed regime finally fell in April 1992, outliving the Soviet Union itself, which disintegrated in 1991. In its dying months, the USSR finally reached agreement with the USA that both sides would halt arms supplies to their respective protégés, the Najibullah government and the Mujahidin.

Over the 1989–92 period, the government had controlled the cities of Kabul, Mazar-i-Sharif, Kandahar, Herat and Jalalabad, together with a number of smaller centres, while the Mujahidin were present in the countryside, attacking government positions and launching rocket attacks on the capital. The government's capacity to stay in power was in large part due to the resources provided by the Soviet Union, which enabled it both to defend its urban strongholds and to provide the urban populations with a reasonable level of income. In addition, it was able to buy support in the rural areas, including the services of various militia groups, such as that of Rashid Dostam in northern Afghanistan. When the resources ran out, Najibullah was vulnerable to the many other power-seekers lurking in the wings.

The Najibullah regime also benefited from growing fragmentation within the ranks of the Mujahidin. The relative unity they had shown during the period of Soviet occupation quickly evaporated following the departure of Soviet troops. The rural areas became far more dangerous than they had been for years as the old solidarity that had held the many elements of the Mujahidin together gave way to factionalism and banditry. Localised fighting erupted between members of one Mujahidin group and another, pitting village against village, neighbour against neighbour and brother against brother. The traditional mediation structures of village elders strove with varying degrees of success to bring an end to each outbreak of fighting. However, the overtures made by the Najibullah government to Mujahidin commanders and traditional leaders throughout the country further undermined the unity of the movement.

The situation in Peshawar was not much better. The city became a place of constant fear, with Afghan liberals and aid workers becoming particular targets of fringe movements taking anti-Western positions from an Islamist perspective. Assassinations of intellectuals were frequent. At least one aid worker disappeared, and others left in response to death threats. A riot in one of the refugee camps, in April 1990, destroyed all the premises of a major agency after local mullahs had accused it of trying to convert widows to Christianity.

The fall of the Najibullah government in April 1992 served as the legitimate end to the jihad and prompted a large-scale return of refugees from Pakistan and, to a lesser extent, from Iran. The rate of return, which had been extremely low during the preceding years, accelerated to a rush as 1.2 million refugees returned from Pakistan over a six-month period during the spring, summer and early autumn of 1992. By the beginning of 1994, the number in Pakistan had fallen to 1.47 million out of the original 3.2 million and the number in Iran had fallen to 1.85 million out of the original 2.9 million.

The continued existence of the jihad was, almost certainly, the dominant factor in the earlier reluctance to return, although insecurity and economic factors would have had some impact. It is also likely that the Mujahidin parties actively discouraged refugees from returning from the camps until the creation of an Islamic government in Kabul, and that it would have been in their interests for their followers to return to Afghanistan as soon as the Najibullah government fell, in order to strengthen their respective power bases inside the country. However, in doing this the parties ran the risk that the refugees, once free of the camp environment, might assert their independence. While the refugees were subject to the control of the parties, it should not be assumed that they submitted passively to the wishes of the parties or their backers. For the vast majority of refugees, the jihad justified the move into exile and a return could not be countenanced until the jihad had ended. The decisions were, for the most part, spontaneous and freely taken.

The fall of Najibullah had been preceded by the desertion of the powerful northern militia leader from the Uzbek area of northern Afghanistan, Rashid Dostam. Dostam's forces, highly distinctive with their long hair and calf-length trousers, had a reputation for ferocity and had been an important element in the success of Najibullah's troops in their battles with the Mujahidin between 1989 and 1992. When Dostam did a deal with Masoud, which also included senior figures from Najibullah's government, the stage was set for the armed but peaceful entry of the Mujahidin into Kabul on 25 April 1992. An attempt to whisk Najibullah quietly out of the country was foiled at Kabul airport and he was forced to return to the capital, where he sought refuge with the UN and was accommodated in one of its compounds.

The calm takeover of Kabul was extremely short-lived. Hekmatyar, angry that he had not got what he wanted from the power-sharing deal, resorted to arms in an effort to strengthen his position and provoked a civil war that played itself out, Beirut style, on the streets of Kabul. For months there were road-blocks on every street corner, Kabul was carved up into territories controlled by different groups, and law and order were virtually non-existent.

Efforts were made to legitimise the regime through discussions sponsored by Pakistan between the seven member parties of the Afghan Interim Government. The first interim president, Sibghatullah Mujadidi, assisted by Masoud as defence minister, did what he could to bring the situation under control. When Rabbani came to power after the first three months, he took the process further but had to deal with continuing hostilities between the Shi'a Hisb-e-Wahdat and the Saudi-backed Ittihad-i-Islami forces. However, following a major rocket attack on Kabul in August 1992, which killed more than 1,800 civilians and led large numbers to flee north to Mazar-i-Sharif, and after further heavy fighting in January and February 1993, it proved necessary to negotiate a new power-sharing arrangement under which Rabbani remained as president and Hekmatyar became prime minister. The latter called a meeting at his base at Charasyab, south of the capital, to pick a cabinet, but Rabbani was shot at on his way there and had to turn back. Hekmatyar did not feel safe entering the city and so had to rule in name only.

The heavy street-fighting between Sayyaf's Ittihad-i-Islami forces and those of Hisb-e-Wahdat, which had occupied western Kabul when Najibullah fell, took its toll on both the inhabitants and their homes and many left the city for the countryside or Iran or fled to the nearby southern suburbs. Masoud's forces eventually joined in on the side of Ittihad, and both parties launched a fierce onslaught on western Kabul in February 1993 in what came to be known as the Afshar massacre.

It is not clear how Masoud got himself into this position. It is likely that he was mindful of the fact that the Mujahidin government had come to power through an alliance of Tajiks and Uzbeks. He was therefore concerned not to alienate the Pushtuns, perhaps remembering the fate of the only Tajik leader to have taken power in Kabul, Habibullah II, who was overthrown by the Pushtun establishment in 1929 after less than a year as ruler. Sayyaf, a Pushtun, was thus a useful ally and it is likely that he also provided access to Saudi funds. However, Masoud then found himself opposing the Hazaras, who would have been the more natural allies given the long-standing resentment in the north against Pushtun domination over the preceding decades, from which the Hazaras had suffered particularly. It is of interest that it is this alliance of Uzbeks, Hazaras and Tajiks that is now opposing the Pushtun Taliban at the time of writing, in October 2001.

Masoud had particular difficulties with Hekmatyar. The tensions between the two men went back some way, and it proved difficult to come to an accommodation that would ensure a share of power between all the main elements within Afghanistan. Masoud accused Hekmatyar of being a tool of Pakistan's strategic interests in Afghanistan and saw any arrangement with him as providing an opening for Pakistani colonisation. Hekmatyar wanted ultimate power in Afghanistan, and viewed Masoud as a major obstacle to this ambition.

Whatever Rabbani's and Masoud's calculations as to how best to achieve a broad-based Islamic government in Afghanistan, they succeeded in alienating the Uzbeks as well as finding themselves engaged in battle with the Hazaras. Dostam, having played a key role in the fall of Najibullah, was hoping for a share of power in Kabul. He consistently argued for a federal system of government, in which the regions would have a high degree of autonomy, but was continually sidelined. In December 1992 Rabbani had himself re-elected as president by a hand-picked national assembly, demonstrating a clear lack of regard for Dostam as well as the other leaders. Relations deteriorated over the following year. Finally, on 1 January 1994, rockets rained on Kabul as Dostam and Hekmatyar joined forces to try to unseat Rabbani. The attempt failed, but it spread panic amongst the population and led to the exodus of over 65,000 people to Pakistan and to other parts of Afghanistan. Hekmatyar continued to rocket the capital for the rest of 1994, pushing the number of those fleeing the capital to 300,000, but he was not able to make any progress in his efforts to take power.

March 1995 saw the expulsion of Hekmatyar from his base at Charasyab at the hands of the Taliban, and the simultaneous removal of Hisb-e-Wahdat as an effective force in Kabul. For the first time since the Mujahidin takeover of April 1992, Kabul was out of rocket range and the city experienced a period of calm that attracted the return of aid agencies in force. Their assistance was much needed over the winter as simultaneous blockades by the Taliban and Hekmatyar (from his other base at Sarobi, astride the main Kabul–Jalalabad road) provoked a major humanitarian crisis in response to food and fuel shortages.

After continued calls for Rabbani to accede to peace deals proposed by the UN and others, providing for a handover of power to an interim government, Rabbani and Masoud finally negotiated a deal with Hekmatyar whereby the latter would become prime minister in a new government of national unity. Dostam, who had up to that point been in alliance with Hekmatyar and Hisb-e-Wahdat, was not impressed by the new arrangement and rejected appeals that he also join. However, Rabbani, Masoud and Hekmatyar managed to govern for a few months before they were ousted by the Taliban. Hekmatyar marked his brief period in office by cautiously introducing a number of policies aimed at increasing the conformity of the population to what he regarded as Islamic requirements. However, these were not as stringent as those subsequently applied by the Taliban.

While developments took their course in Kabul over the 1992–96 period, the rest of the country operated as separate fiefdoms, each experiencing very different conditions. In Herat, the Jamiat resistance leader, Ismail Khan, took control as soon as the Najibullah government fell in April 1992. He was able to create the necessary conditions for three years of stability and growing prosperity, which ended only with the Taliban takeover of the province in September 1995. Mazar, under Dostam, was almost as stable, albeit with more guns in evidence. The Ismailis, who, in alliance with Dostam, controlled Pul-i-Khumri and the main highway north of the Salang Pass, had reached an accommodation with local Mujahidin commanders, which kept the peace for most of the time. The Tajik north-east, amidst the ascending Pamir mountains, continued with a reasonably settled existence under Jamiat control. The eastern provinces, by contrast, were held together by an uneasy alliance of Mujahidin parties brought together in the Nangarhar *shura* under the leadership of Haji Qadir. Tensions were never far below the surface, and isolated incidents such as the unexplained assassination of four UN staff members in February 1993 served to remind observers of the fragility of the situation. However, further south, the border town of Khost had managed to cohere around a collective Mujahidin leadership after its capture in March 1991 and to attract substantial aid. Ghazni, to the south-west of Khost, also found a leader, Qari Babar, under whom it could unite. Yet Gardez, between the two, defied all efforts to bring order. It was none the less a haven of peace compared with Kandahar, which experienced virtual anarchy from 1992 until the Taliban takeover as the various Mujahidin commanders fought for control of the streets and reduced much of the city to rubble.

The so-called Mujahidin Government of the Islamic State of Afghanistan was thus simply a coalition government made up of an amalgam of the seven political parties that had previously formed the Afghan Interim Government. As already mentioned, this government-in-exile resulted from the decision by the Pakistan government, backed by the USA, to channel resources to the resistance movement in Afghanistan through a limited number of organisations. The more powerful three of the seven organisations selected had their origins in the Islamist movement that had emerged in Kabul University from the late 1950s. The US government had therefore, in its efforts to undermine the Soviet Union, created a government in Afghanistan that had its roots among a small group of radicals in the elite circles of the university, and had replaced the minority government of the PDPA with another minority government. The relatively weak position of the three traditionalist parties within the government meant that it was never able to establish much of a power base in the countryside, except, perhaps, in the north-east, where Jamiat held control. Rabbani's hopes of building grass-roots support never materialised beyond these areas: his Tajik origins made it almost impossible, particularly in the Pushtun tribal areas. Furthermore, the government alienated and profoundly disappointed the broad mass of the population in the Pushtun belt – who might otherwise have been persuaded by its Islamic credentials – through the constant struggles for power that characterised its period in government. The way was thus left open for the Taliban to create a popular movement.

4 The Warriors of God

It appears that the Taliban began as a small spontaneous group in Kandahar, perhaps in early 1994. Its members, who were described as religious students, are said to have felt outrage at the behaviour of the Mujahidin leaders fighting for power in the city and to have decided to take action to end what they saw as corrupt practices, drawing on Islam as a justification for their intervention.

How they moved from small group to major force is not clear. However, it is thought likely that they were seen by elements outside Afghanistan as being potentially useful in promoting their various interests, and that these elements decided it was worthwhile to provide them with some backing. The nature and extent of the backing received from outside has been the subject of much speculation. Pakistan, the USA and Saudi Arabia have all been implicated.

It is none the less clear that they benefited considerably from the willingness of young people, both from the rural areas and from refugee camps on the Pakistan border, to join their ranks as they advanced through southern Afghanistan. They were also able to draw on a significant quantity of weaponry, either abandoned by retreating forces or found in the process of disarming the population.

The ideological underpinning of the movement has been a further cause for debate. There appears to be little doubt that the Islamic *madrasahs* in the refugee camps, where Islam has been taught on the basis of recitation of the Qur'an, have proved to be fertile ground for recruits. It is also likely that the orphanages operated in the refugee camps, with funding from Saudi Arabia, the Gulf States and the Mujahidin parties, will have produced strong adherents to radical Islam, some of whom will have been attracted by the call to arms issued by the Taliban. Also evident is the role of the Islamist parties in Pakistan in training young people in their various educational establishments, and the contribution these establishments have made to the expansion of the Taliban movement. Equally unclear is the question of how the Taliban forces have received their military training.

There has also been much debate as to whether the movement is essentially a Pushtun one, given that an overhelming majority of its supporters have been Pushtun. This has led to speculation that the movement has been supported in an effort to reassert the Pushtun dominance in Afghanistan that existed before the war and was challenged by the control of Kabul by the Tajik leadership of Rabbani and Masoud. The Taliban have insisted that the movement is open to all ethnic groups in Afghanistan and it is clear that some of the adherents are, indeed, non-Pushtuns. The movement is, however, exclusively Sunni in its interpretation of Islam and cannot, therefore, embrace the Shi'as of central Afghanistan or the Ismailis of the north-east.

The absolute leader of the Taliban is Mullah Muhammad Omar, who has been given the supreme religious title of Amir Al-Mu'minin (Leader of the Faithful). He presides over the Kandahar *shura*, which has authority over the *shuras* in other Taliban-controlled areas. Herat has a governor but Kabul is controlled by a six-man *shura*, presided over by the president of the *shura*, and by a number of government ministers. Decision-making within the Taliban is reported to be by consensus. There is, therefore, a tendency for more conservative elements to prevail.

Mullah Omar is a Pushtun from south-western Afghanistan. He was previously a member of one of the traditionalist Mujahidin parties, Hisb-e-Islami, headed by Younis Khalis. He acquired a reputation as a brilliant commander and lost an eye in fighting against the Soviet forces. He is said to be in his late thirties or early forties. An aura of mystery surrounds Mullah Omar, because he is rarely seen in public or by visiting dignitaries. He limits his contacts to a few close associates, including the governors he has appointed, and is said to give his time exclusively to the organisation of the Taliban's military campaign. He often leaves the tasks associated with relating to the outside world, including meetings with heads of state and the UN secretary-general's special envoy, to his subordinates. He is said to be pious and to live very simply.

The movement depends very heavily on the continued commitment of its footsoldiers, some of whom will have already seen friends martyr themselves for the cause. Particular care has to be taken not to move too far in the direction of liberal, urban or Western values, lest the footsoldiers feel that they have been betrayed and withdraw the support on which the drive to take the whole country relies.

The Taliban have little experience in running a government administration, nor did they see this as a priority when they took power. They have demonstrated enormous single-mindedness in focusing on the military campaign, on the eradication of corruption and on the achievement of law and order. The maintenance and strengthening of administrative structures have been very much secondary concerns.

The capture of Kabul has brought a new entity, known as the Department for the Promotion of Virtue and the Prevention of Vice, to prominence. These religious police have played an increasing role in enforcing the Taliban policies on the urban populations. However, their actions have often contravened the policies of other elements of the Taliban leadership, leading to confusion and to speculation as to a possible struggle between hardliners and relative moderates within the movement.

The Taliban appeared to emerge out of nowhere when they first came to the world's notice in October 1994. Their arrival on the Afghan military scene coincided with an initiative by the government of Pakistan to dispatch a trade convoy through Afghanistan, via Kandahar and Herat, to Turkmenistan. As the convoy entered Afghanistan, travelling north from Quetta, it was attacked by an armed group. Immediately, another group came to the rescue and fought off the attackers. These were the Taliban.

After allowing the convoy to proceed, the Taliban moved on Kandahar and took the city with almost no resistance. Kandahar had witnessed virtual anarchy for the previous two years, as a number of Mujahidin groups fought for control. The Taliban were able to seize the faction leaders, killing some and imprisoning others. Having taken the city, they called on the population to surrender their weapons at a designated place and to cooperate with the new authorities in bringing peace to the area. The people duly complied.

The Taliban simultaneously announced that it was their mission to

free Afghanistan of its existing corrupt leadership and to create a society
that accorded with Islam. They issued decrees in which they required
men to wear turbans, beards, short hair and *shalwar kameez* and women
to wear the *burqa*, a garment that covers the entire body, including the
face. Men were strongly encouraged to pray five times a day, ideally in
the mosque. Women were advised that it was their responsibility to bring
up the next generation of Muslims. To this end, they were prohibited
from working. It was also made clear that the education of girls would
have to await the drawing up of an appropriate Islamic curriculum by
religious scholars, and that this process could start only when the Taliban
had control of the whole country. Other decrees banned music, games
and any representation of the human or animal form. In order to enforce
these bans, televisions and tapes were symbolically displayed in public
places.

The remarkable success of the Taliban in bringing order to Kandahar earned them considerable popularity and this, building on popular
superstition and combined with their distinctive white turbans and
obvious religious fervour and purity, lent them an almost supernatural
aura. When they moved westwards from Kandahar, their reputation
had already travelled before them and they were able to clear the main
road of armed groups and bandits with great ease. As they captured
positions they seized abandoned weaponry, some of it left in great haste,
and encouraged people to join the ranks of their fighters.

Over the winter of 1994–95, the Taliban were able to repeat this
pattern many times over and, by February 1995, they were positioned
on hilltops overlooking the southern suburbs of Kabul, having taken
almost half of Afghanistan. They had even managed to secure the
speedy evacuation of Charasyab, to the south of the capital, from which
Gulbuddin Hekmatyar had launched rockets on the city for three years.
As they approached Kabul from the south-west they captured the western suburbs at the invitation of the Shi'a group, Hisb-e-Wahdat, which
feared a worse outcome if Masoud's forces were to attack. In the course
of the military operation the Shi'a leader, Abdul Ali Mazari, was taken
by the Taliban and he died a few days later in their custody, for reasons
that remain unclear.

The occupation of western Kabul proved to be short-lived, however.
Government troops launched a major offensive and were able to retake

the area within a month of its capture by the Taliban. They were also able to push the Taliban out of Charasyab to positions out of rocket range of Kabul. Thereafter, there was a virtual stalemate between the forces of the Taliban and those of the government, at least in relation to Kabul, until September 1996. During the intervening 18 months, the capital experienced a period of relative calm until the Taliban were able to recover Charasyab and also capture new positions in October 1995. These enabled them to shell and rocket the city while Hekmatyar's troops simultaneously blocked commercial and aid convoys from the east. The northern route to Mazar-i-Sharif also remained closed, due to the long-standing conflict between the government and Dostam.

The winter of 1995–96 was a particularly harsh one for Kabul as food and fuel shortages and spiralling inflation took their toll on a highly impoverished people. Humanitarian agencies pulled out the stops to get relief supplies to the capital, but the task was far from easy. Memories of this hardship were a factor in the relative ease with which the Taliban subsequently took Kabul in September 1996.

While the Taliban were endeavouring to take Kabul, there was also intense military activity in western Afghanistan. The city of Herat was, as noted earlier, under the control of Ismail Khan, who was allied to the government. He had taken Herat Province in April 1992, when the Soviet-backed government had fallen, and had gradually increased his dominion or influence over the western provinces of Farah and Nimroz, to the south, and Badghis, to the north-west. When the Taliban moved west from Kandahar, they sought to take the entire road through Herat to the Turkmenistan border. However, their way was blocked at Shindand, about 120 km south of Herat, where there was a large military airbase. Ismail Khan's forces mined the approaches to the airbase in an effort to withstand the forward advance of the Taliban. They were succesful in holding off the attack, but had to contend with a wave of men willing to martyr themselves for the cause as they rushed forward over the minefields. This aspect of Taliban strategy added further to the image of invincibility that went before them.

Over the ensuing months, there was a stand-off between the forces of the Taliban and Ismail Khan at Delaram, on the border between the provinces of Farah and Helmand. Then, in August 1995, Ismail Khan's forces took the initiative and advanced towards Kandahar. They moved with remarkable speed at first and posed a serious threat to the city. However, they were halted by the Taliban at Girishk, about 120 km west of Kandahar, and then pushed back. The Taliban kept going and, within a relatively short space of time, had taken Shindand and walked into Herat without a fight, entering it on 5 September 1995. Based on prior agreement between the Taliban and Dostam, the latter's forces lent air support to the advance.

There has been much speculation as to why Ismail Khan gave in so easily to the Taliban and effectively handed over Herat to them. Rumours at the time that there had been differences between Ismail Khan and the central government in Kabul, which had led to Ismail Khan's resignation or dismissal from the post of governor, cannot be substantiated. Another rumour in circulation was that Ismail Khan wished to avoid the destruction of a city he had taken three years to rebuild and that he may not have felt able to count on the support of the population who, having enjoyed a period of peace, were reluctant to take up arms again. The fact that the Taliban had, up to that point, a reputation for behaving relatively well when taking new areas – they did not engage in looting, rape or mindless destruction – may have strengthened an assessment that resistance by the population on any scale could not be relied upon.

When the Taliban took Herat they issued edicts on the dress and behaviour of the population, as they had done in Kandahar, ordered the closure of all the girls' schools, and placed a ban on women working. The statue of a horse in the city centre was decapitated because, by representing the animal form, it was seen as being inconsistent with Islam. The Taliban conducted house-to-house searches to disarm the population.

The edicts relating to female access to education and employment had a greater impact than they had had in Kandahar. In Kandahar, the administrative infrastructure had effectively collapsed by the time the Taliban arrived and there were few girls' schools in operation. There were also very few opportunities for women to seek employment outside the home. However, in Herat city in 1994 there was a reported school population of 21,663 girls and 23,347 boys. By contrast, in the rural areas, 1,940 girls were attending school as compared with 74,620 boys (Save the Children Fund UK, 1994). A significant proportion of the teachers were women and it proved necessary to close many boys' schools as a result. Further, much of the population of Herat had lived as refugees in Iran, where female access to education had been provided as a right. The bans on girls being educated, pending the introduction of a new and more appropriate curriculum, and on women working, therefore had a significant impact.

The capture of Herat by the Taliban was felt to be a military occupation, not only because of the restrictions placed on female access to education and employment but also because, culturally and linguistically, the predominantly Pushtun and rural Taliban were very different from the Persian-speaking Heratis, with their long aesthetic and liberal traditions.

During the early months of Taliban rule in Herat, long queues were reported outside the Iranian consulate as large numbers applied for visas for Iran. Many of these were educated professionals, a proportion of whom had been working in the various government ministries. There was an obvious slowing down in the construction sector, reducing the opportunities for people to engage in daily labouring work and accelerating the process of return to Iran. The repatriation programme from Iran to western Afghanistan ground to a standstill.

Humanitarian agencies sought to engage in dialogue with the Taliban in Herat as they had done in Kandahar. In the latter city, it had proved possible to secure authority for women to work in the health sector and this authority had been extended when the Taliban took Herat. However, the agencies in Herat were not able to achieve any modification of the ban on women working in non-health-related posts or a reversal of the closure of girls' schools.

Following the capture of Herat the Taliban made few gains until, a year later, they suddenly marched into Jalalabad, on 11 September 1996. Again, there was minimal resistance as the Mujahidin leaders who had composed the Nangarhar *shura* opted to leave without much of a fight. The Taliban then surprised all observers by forcing themselves through the apparently impenetrable Sarobi Gorge. After a few days of intense fighting in the eastern suburbs of Kabul, they walked into the capital on 26 September with scarcely a shot being fired. Shockwaves were then felt throughout the world when ex-President Najibullah and his brother, who was visiting him, were seized from the protection of the UN compound, within a few hours of the Taliban entering the city, and hanged in a public place. It is still not known whether this hanging was authorised by the Taliban leadership or carried out spontaneously by enthusiastic followers, or whether others, with old scores to settle, took the opportunity created by the situation to wreak their revenge. It was rumoured that the atrocity arose from old antagonisms within the PDPA. Others wondered whether Najibullah's years as head of the secret police had played a part.

The population of Kabul would, by this stage, have been apprehensive of a further prolonged siege of the capital. Many had already sold even their most basic possessions and were nearing destitution. When the Taliban entered there was therefore considerable relief and a hope that there might, at last, be peace and the possibility of an improvement in the local economy. It is likely that Rabbani and Masoud were aware of this view amongst the population, and this may have been a factor in their decision not to fight for every last inch of Kabul. The aura of invincibility held by the Taliban may have created an additional concern that the government forces would be unwilling to put up a fight. The government may also have calculated that opposition to the Taliban would grow once they had taken the capital, and Masoud made this view explicit in a number of subsequent statements.

However, the Taliban did not wait to consolidate their hold on Kabul but moved immediately north. Within a few days they were facing Dostam's troops at the top of the Salang Pass, which divides north from south Afghanistan, and Masoud's forces at the entrance to the Panjshir Valley, which had witnessed much of the resistance to the Soviet occupation. The Taliban sought to negotiate a peace deal with Dostam. Dostam and Masoud responded by opting to shelve their long-standing enmity and to form a military alliance; their combined forces were then able to push the Taliban back to positions just north of Kabul, where a new stalemate developed.

The Taliban responded to the alliance by opening up a new front in north-western Afghanistan. In October 1996 they took Badghis Province, which Dostam had seized in September 1995 following the Taliban capture of Herat. Heavy fighting ensued between the forces of Dostam and the Taliban in eastern Badghis. The population of Herat were said to be apprehensive of a Dostam victory because of the reputation of Dostam's forces for looting and raping in the wake of battle.

In Kabul, the Taliban proceeded to issue the same edicts as they had done in Kandahar and Herat. However, it soon became clear that there was to be a greater degree of enforcement of the Taliban requirements, particularly that men should pray at their local mosques rather than individually and that the dress codes for men and women, including long beards, *shalwar kameez* and turbans for men and the *burqa* for women, should be strictly observed.

There was also a downturn in the economy as there had been in Herat. This was in spite of easier access for trade than there had been during the previous siege of Kabul (mitigated by Hekmatyar entering the government a few weeks before the Taliban takeover), and in contrast to the mushrooming of the Kandahar economy during the post-Taliban period. In the case of Kabul, this may have been a consequence of many government servants suddenly losing their jobs or being paid only very irregularly when the Taliban took control. The departure, with the ousted government, of what little was left of the more affluent element of Kabul society may have accelerated this process. Certainly the Kabul money market, which provides a good indicator of the health of the economy, responded very positively to the Taliban takeover during the first week or so, but the afghani then fell in value again. Subsequent problems, with Dostam printing his own banknotes and the ousted government flooding the market with newly printed notes, caused spiralling inflation and a virtual collapse of the afghani.

Whether for economic reasons or fear of renewed conflict, there was a significant outward flow of people from Jalalabad and Kabul following the arrival of the Taliban. Ten thousand people left for Pakistan from Jalalabad in September 1996, some in direct response to a bombing raid launched by government forces. A further 50,000 fled to Pakistan from Kabul between October and December 1996 in response to Taliban restrictions and a growing climate of fear. Provision was made for the new arrivals at Nasir Bagh camp near Peshawar. As in Herat, this departure further weakened the government and reduced the pool of skilled professionals able to run an administration.

During the early months after the takeover of Kabul, the Taliban gave every indication of having overextended themselves. It proved difficult for outside organisations and diplomatic missions to be clear as to the nature of the internal decision-making process. There were inconsistencies in some of the public statements made, which created concern and confusion. Some of the soldiers in the streets appeared to be acting in the absence of any clear chain of command.

It was also evident that the Taliban regarded the population of Kabul as being very different from those living in other conquered areas. Many of them had their roots in rural traditions and gave the impression of seeing Kabul as corrupt and decadent. The behaviour of the foot-soldiers at times reflected this attitude, and led to a number of incidents on which Amnesty International reported. The Taliban leadership gave every indication that they regretted these early excesses and Mullah Omar, the Taliban leader in Kandahar, issued an appeal on Radio Voice of Shari'a for his followers to treat the population of Kabul kindly.

There were also tensions in Kabul arising from Ahmed Shah Ma-soud's statements that he hoped the population would rise up against the Taliban. The Taliban were reported to have conducted house-to-house searches for those rumoured to be sympathetic to Masoud, and a number of people were arrested. Because of the absence of records as to who was held where, there was concern over apparent disappearances.

Three months after their capture of Kabul, the Taliban made an-other attempt to move north. This time they were successful in taking the settlements between Kabul and the Salang Pass, but they avoided some of the problems they had faced from insurrections during their earlier attempt by evacuating the area. Over a hundred thousand people were sent to Kabul as refugees while the Taliban consolidated their hold.

As 1997 took its course the numbers entering Kabul from the north rose gradually to 200,000. These had to fend largely for themselves, staying with relatives or finding some way of surviving. Appeals were made by the United Nations High Commissioner for Refugees for people to be allowed to return to their homes north of the capital, but these were rejected. The Taliban were totally focused on their objective of taking the whole country and did not want to take any risks.

The early months of 1997 were characterised by a stalemate as fighting continued on a number of fronts. To the south of the Salang Pass, Hisb-e-Wahdat withstood the efforts of the Taliban to cross the Shibar Pass and so move west and then north over an alternative route to the blocked Salang Pass. Masoud's forces also kept the Taliban busy in and around the Panjshir Valley, to the east. Casualties on both sides were said to be high. In the north-west of Afghanistan, at Ghormach in Badghis, the fighting was said to be even more intense as the Taliban attempted to move into Dostam's territory. The Taliban even encountered problems in the area they had already conquered as Haji Qadir, the ousted leader of the former Nangarhar *shura*, organised an incursionary movement from Pakistan into Kunar and Nangarhar until he was expelled by Pakistan on 14 May.

This stalemate was suddenly and dramatically broken when one of Dostam's generals, Abdul Malik, who controlled the province of Faryab to the immediate east of the Badghis front-line, announced on 19 May that he had defected to the Taliban. He then moved on Mazar and took it, without a fight, on 24 May, Dostam having fled to Uzbekistan. The following day he allowed the Taliban to enter the city.

The Taliban leadership responded quickly to the victory by sending many of their top people to Mazar. The first country to announce that it had decided to recognise the Taliban as the legitimate government of Afghanistan was Pakistan, which promptly dispatched an ambassador. Saudi Arabia and the United Arab Emirates quickly followed Pakistan's example and accorded the Taliban recognition.

There were also reports coming in from the provinces of Kunduz, Baghlan and Takhar, further east, of commanders changing allegiance to the Taliban. It looked as though nothing could stop their onward advance or thwart their ambition to take the country. Further evidence of this was provided by the announced defection of another opposition commander, this time one of Masoud's men who controlled the Salang Pass. On 27 May, he permitted the Taliban to move foward to the top of the pass and then proceed through the Salang Tunnel at its peak. As the last soldiers entered the tunnel was blown up behind them, preventing their return.

This immediately provoked rumours of treachery and these were reinforced when, on the same day, the population of Mazar turned on the Taliban. However, the events in Mazar are not so easily consistent with an act of treachery. They started with Taliban attempts to disarm the population and with their particular response to the resistance put up by a Hisb-e-Wahdat group in the city. As additional Taliban arrived to punish this group they were set upon by the people of the neighbourhood, and very quickly the whole population seemed to rise up. The Taliban spread themselves throughout the city in an effort to bring the situation under control and were cut down one by one. It is very difficult to gain a clear picture of how many Taliban were killed on that day, but witnesses spoke of a period of total anarchy and slaughter.

The Taliban were in shock, but their forces – now on the north flank of the Salang Pass – moved forward undeterred and proceeded to take the Ismaili-held settlements of Khenjan and Doshi and the industrial town of Pul-i-Khumri. They then joined up with the rump of the Taliban forces who had escaped from Mazar at a point halfway between Mazar and Pul-i-Khumri. Gradually, over the following days, they were pushed back by Abdul Malik's forces from the west, by the Ismaili forces from the south and by Masoud's forces from the east until Pul-i-Khumri was retaken on 11 June. The remaining Taliban then fled north to the welcome of the long-established Pushtun population of Baghlan and Kunduz. In the meantime, Masoud's forces had succeeded in taking Jabal-us-Seraj, at the southern entrance of the Salang Pass, from the Taliban on 29 May. The Taliban responded very quickly with a fierce counter-attack, but were unable to do much more than dent the positions of the opposition forces.

All went quiet for a while as the Taliban took stock of the situation. Skirmishes continued with Hisb-e-Wahdat forces and there were confused reports from Kunduz and Badghis regarding the relative gains of the opposing armies. The four elements of the northern alliance, namely the forces of Abdul Malik, Masoud, Hisb-e-Wahdat and the Ismailis, gave every appearance of cohering as an effective political and military entity, although the law and order situation on the urban streets was far from good.

Then, on 20 July, the opposition alliance succeeded in capturing Charikar and the strategically important airbase of Bagram, north of Kabul. Further gains were made until the Taliban managed to halt the northern forces 25 km north of the capital, where a stalemate ensued. These military successes made the Taliban increasingly nervous at the possibility of insurrection within the capital and they stepped up their arrests of possible opposition sympathisers. The Persian-speaking Tajik and Hazara populations, who represent a sizeable proportion of the Kabuli population, became the inevitable targets for these arrests.

Similar arrests of Hazaras were rumoured to have taken place in Herat, in response to reports of military manoeuvres by Iranian forces on the other side of the border. The increasing public accusations by the Taliban, following the May débâcle in Mazar, that Iran had been providing support to the northern alliance were therefore matched by a growing ethnic and religious element to the conflict as the Shi'a Hazaras of Afghanistan found themselves engaged in ever-deepening conflict with the Taliban.

From early August 1997, there were rumours of fragmentation within the ranks of the northern alliance. On 8 September the Taliban forces in Kunduz took advantage of a defection by a local commander in Tashkurgan, which sits astride the main Mazar to Pul-i-Khumri road, to launch an attack on Mazar airport. This coincided with a collapse of authority within Mazar as Abdul Malik departed and the city became parcelled up between Hisb-e-Wahdat, Jamiat and two opposing elements within the Uzbek camp, one affiliated to Abdul Malik and the other to the ousted Rashid Dostam. However, the Hisb-e-Wahdat forces appeared to dominate the military scene and proceeded to loot the offices of humanitarian agencies, stripping them bare. When Dostam suddenly appeared in Afghanistan on 12 September, having made his way from Turkey, it was not at all clear whether he would be able to regain control of the situation. While he grouped his forces outside Mazar, the Taliban proceeded to encircle the city as September came to an end. However, somehow it proved possible for the northern forces to resist the Taliban attack and push the Taliban all the way back to Kunduz before the in-fighting between Abdul Malik and Dostam started again. The additional defeat increased the nervousness of the Taliban yet further, and they tightened their grip on the populations of Kabul and Herat. This further dampened economic activity as men became increasingly scared to venture out onto the streets.

In August 1998, the Taliban made another attempt on Mazar-i-Sharif, on this occasion facilitated by disunity within the ranks of the opposition. Their successful capture of the city was accompanied by a news blackout so that no journalists were able to witness or report what happened. However, from reports submitted by the UNHCR, Amnesty International and Human Rights Watch, and statements issued by the Iranian government, it is almost certain that they killed large numbers of Hazaras, possibly thousands, as an act of revenge for the Hazara uprising against them when they entered Mazar in May 1997 and the subsequent massacre of 2,000 Taliban prisoners by Abdul Malik's forces. In addition, eight Iranian diplomats and an Iranian journalist based in Mazar were killed. As the Taliban subsequently advanced on the Hazara stronghold of Bamyan the following month, the Taliban leader responded to concerns expressed by Amnesty International for the security of the Hazara population there by stating that he had ordered his soldiers to treat civilians and prisoners properly, thus acknowledging, implicitly, that they had not done so in Mazar. Reports were mixed as to how restrained the Taliban forces were in their successful capture of Bamyan on this occasion, but it is clear that the city has been reduced to rubble as the Taliban and Hisb-e-Wahdat have since fought for control of it and that both sides have had scant regard for the population affected by the conflict.

No further gains were made by the Taliban until September 2000, when they captured Taloqan in north-east Afghanistan, leading to the exodus of 170,000 people to Pakistan and the displacement of a further 80,000 within the area. They faced continuing resistance to their efforts to capture the remaining corner of the country, including the opening up of new fronts by the opposition in areas already under Taliban control. The Taliban were said to be facing increasing difficulties recruiting within Afghanistan and were resorting to forced recruitment, as were the opposition forces. Young men were reported to be making their way to Pakistan, Iran and beyond to escape such conscription. The Taliban were also accused by opposition forces of relying heavily on volunteers from Pakistani *madrasahs*, both Pakistanis and Afghan, and from other parts of the Islamic world. For whatever reason, the Taliban-led forces appeared to be behaving more punitively when they recovered territory lost to the opposition in the many clashes that occurred, often burning houses and bazaars. Of particular note was the massacre of more than one hundred civilians, reported on by the UN secretary-general and Amnesty International, which followed the temporary recapture of Yakawlang in central Afghanistan from Hisb-e-Wahdat in early January 2001. Also of note was the burning of the centre of Yakawlang some months later after a period of oscillating control.

The assassination of Ahmed Shah Masoud in early September 2001 might have been the precursor to a planned major offensive by the Taliban to capture the remaining area of the country under opposition control, in the north-east, but the terrorist attacks in the USA of September 11 will have diverted the attention of both the Taliban and their supporters to more urgent concerns and no such initiative has been taken.

5 The Taliban Creed

The Western vision of Islam is firmly anchored in the crusades, with images of holy warriors, fired with the passion of martyrs, storming the battlements of some crusader castle. Within the Western psyche there appears to be an almost paranoid fear of Islam as something wild, mindless and potentially overwhelming. As attitudes towards women have changed within Western society, particularly during the present century, there has also been a perception of Islam as a religion that is oppressive towards women.

In the 'New World Order' of the post-Soviet period the Islamic world is fast taking on the role of the new enemy, with Iran, until recently, assuming the symbolic lead in the eyes of the USA, at least. The Western media have created simplistic images of Muslims as terrorists and oppressors through the catch-all term 'Islamic fundamentalists'. Osama bin Laden has been presented as a hate figure in the US media since the attacks on the US embassies in Nairobi and Dar es Salaam without presenting conclusive evidence of this involvement to the international community. When the World Trade Center and the Pentagon were the targets of even more horrific terrorist attacks on September 11, 2001, the US government immediately claimed that Osama bin Laden was behind this, before they had begun their investigations. This was in spite of the fact that, when a federal government building was blown up in Oklahoma in 1995, the US government had to admit that initial reports in the world's press that Islamic terrorists were suspected were premature and that a group of white Americans linked to a particular cult were now the prime suspects.

In talking about the Taliban, we therefore have to be careful not to fall into the trap of reinforcing negative stereotypes. This is particularly difficult when much of what they have said and done has, if anything, tended to emphasise these very stereotypes. They have emerged on the

scene as holy warriors, overwhelming much of the country through the
onward march of young men willing to martyr themselves for the cause.
They have also, from a Western point of view, and from the point of
view of most Muslims, behaved in an extremely oppressive way towards
women by enforcing their seclusion from society.

Yet they were welcomed when they captured the southern provinces
of Afghanistan and remained popular for some time after their emergence in the refugee camps in Pakistan and with many other Afghans
in exile. Thus, while the people of Herat and Kabul have clearly found
their puritanical values difficult to tolerate, they have had no shortage
of recruits and have had relatively solid backing from tribal and village
elders throughout the south, as well as sympathy from many Afghans
outside the country who felt they were, until the destruction of the
Buddhas of Bamyan in February 2001, an improvement on what went
before. It is therefore important to try to understand the origins of
their beliefs and attitudes.

We could perhaps start by asking why religious and political movements emerge at all, and by tentatively making the observation that
dissatisfaction with the status quo is normally the spur to action.
Typically, a charismatic leader will arise with a vision as to how society
could be made better. A set of principles will be identified to guide
followers, and these will include a code of ethics. In Islam and Christianity, the principles have been given the sanction of a supreme deity.
In secular ideologies, such as socialism, reference is continually made
to the founding theorist. Within each movement, there will inevitably
be differences of view about how to put the belief system into practice
and about how far to compromise in adapting the system to a necessarily
imperfect world.

Like Christianity, Islam has been beset by revivalist movements
aimed at counteracting an apparent backsliding by those in power in
relation to the founding principles recited (in the case of Islam, by
Muhammad) in accordance with divine inspiration. Thus, while the
Reformation in Europe was a response to the growing corruption and
opulence of the Catholic Church, and resulted in the development of
the puritanical Protestant movement, so movements have arisen within
the Islamic world in response to what has been seen as corrupt and
unprincipled behaviour on the part of government. The movements

have generally taken a puritanical form and, as in other parts of the world, there has been a resort to arms to impose the new vision on society.

It may also be useful to consider the relationship between religious movements of a radical or fundamentalist nature and major crises in society. It has been noted that countries affected by chronic civil conflict – often referred to within the humanitarian aid world as complex emergencies – produce Christian and Islamic revivalist movements in which efforts are made to return to what are regarded as the absolute truths of the religion, and to eradicate any influences that have appeared to weaken religious belief.

It could be suggested that this is a response to chaos, an attempt to create a tightly defined framework within which society can be contained, a determined effort to hold back a process by which society is gradually being overwhelmed by potentially destructive forces. There have thus been many examples in both Christianity and Islam of movements emerging that have imposed highly specific codes of conduct and dress on their adherents in order to provide a secure containing environment in what is felt to be a chaotic or overwhelming world. The growth of religious cults is one such response.

The major fear amongst leaders of religious movements has been that the societies to which they belonged would lose their religious beliefs, that the wave of secularism would overtake them. This has been a real fear in the Islamic world ever since the West started to play a dominant role on the world stage, particularly over the last couple of centuries. It has prompted both religious scholars and intellectuals in the Islamic world to reflect on why Western society was able to dominate others, and what this indicated in terms of how Islam might be modified to adapt to new circumstances.

Some have advocated that Islam should seek to incorporate what was seen to be best from Western society while retaining those aspects of Islam that were felt to be superior to what the West had to offer. Others have felt that Islam should be modernised and adapted to the new circumstances in which it found itself, in order to strengthen it *vis-à-vis* the West. Yet others have rejected any kind of accommodation with Western values and have sought to return to the key elements of Islam, at the same time removing all vestiges of Western influence.

Such movements have tended to portray the West in stereotypical terms on a par with those created in the West to refer to the Islamic world.

Negative stereotyping in the West in relation to the Islamic world has, therefore, provoked negative stereotyping of the West by radical Islamic movements. This has, in turn, further hardened the stereotypes created within the West. An interesting consequence of this process is seen in France, where the growth of radical Islam in response to the disadvantages and alienation experienced by the Muslim population has created an ardent defence of secular values by those challenging freedom of religious expression and, in particular, the use of the veil by Muslim women resident in France. Secularism is thus arousing the same fervour as radicalised religion.

Over the centuries, Islamic scholars have debated at length how best to respond to situations that were not envisaged at the time of Muhammad and on which earlier scholars had not pronounced. Each generation of scholars has established new rules to accommodate the unforeseen, drawing on the Qur'an and on the Hadith, the sayings and actions of the Prophet, as reported by his adherents.

Four schools of Islamic or Shari'a law developed, some of which took a more uncompromising stand towards the interpretation of the Qur'an and the Hadith. New movements sprang up, based on Sufist spirituality, in response to the felt need for a personal relationship with the deity. These produced their own ideologies. Islam also incorporated aspects of the cultures it encountered in its forward march – the introduction of the *burqa*, the all-enveloping garment the Taliban are seeking to impose on women, from Turkey into Afghanistan is a good example. There is, as a result, an enormous variety of responses to the Qur'an and the Hadith within the Islamic world, ranging from the relatively liberal societies of Egypt and Jordan to the more puritanical society of Saudi Arabia. In this context, the Taliban can be seen as being at the puritanical end of the spectrum, with parallels in earlier Islamic movements in both Afghanistan and the wider Islamic world (see Chapter 6).

The objectives of the movement were well encapsulated in an interview given by a Taliban spokesman, Mullah Wakil Ahmed, published in the Arabic magazine *Al-Majallah* on 23 October 1996. Asked how and why the Taliban movement had started, he replied:

After the Mujahidin parties came to power in 1992, the Afghan people thought that peace would prevail in the country. However, the leaders began to fight over power in Kabul. Some local leaders, particularly in Kandahar, formed armed gangs that fought each other. There was widespread corruption and theft, and there were road-blocks everywhere. Women were being attacked, raped and killed. Therefore, after these incidents, a group of students from religious schools decided to rise against these leaders in order to alleviate the suffering of the residents of Kandahar Province. We were able to take control of several centres until we reached Kandahar and the former leaders fled from there.

This was the hub of their popular appeal. There had been great hopes when the Soviet-backed government fell in April 1992 that a broad-based Islamic government would be established and that there would at last be peace after 14 years of conflict. In the event, the Mujahidin parties were unable to agree on a power-sharing arrangement amongst themselves or with the militia leader, Rashid Dostam, who controlled the north-central area from Mazar. Furthermore, they had resorted to arms in an effort to resolve the impasse and had subjected the population of Kabul to four years of siege, rocketing and shelling. In Kandahar, there had been total anarchy throughout this period as the different Mujahidin groups fought for supremacy and settled scores. The rural areas of southern Afghanistan had seen similar chaos as one party fought another for local dominance. Traders had had to pay their way through a succession of road-blocks, each held by a different Mujahidin group demanding tolls, and bandits represented an ever-present threat. However, Herat, Mazar and the north-east had been peaceful from 1992 onwards and, for them, the appeal of the Taliban as liberators was less evident.

The aim of the Taliban was the purification of Afghanistan alone. There was no suggestion, at least among the leadership, that they were seeking to spread a particular interpretation of Islam beyond Afghanistan's borders. This view was confirmed by the Taliban Liaison Office in Kandahar, which quoted Mullah Omar as saying that his main goal was to rid Afghanistan of 'corrupt, Western-oriented time-servers'. He was said to have added that foreign relations would be handled later, 'when we have sorted out our own internal affairs'.

Further clarification of the Taliban creed was given in a broadcast by the Taliban's Voice of Shari'a radio station on 5 November 1996:

The Taliban, who have emerged from the masses of the people, have started their struggle to deliver their compatriots from pain and hardship, to ensure complete peace and security across the country by collecting weapons, by doing away with feudal principalities here and there in the country and by creating a powerful Islamic government in Afghanistan.

Mullah Amir Khan Motaqi, the Taliban's acting minister of information and culture, expanded on this creed in a sermon at Friday prayers on 15 November 1996:

There no longer exists any cruelty, oppression, savagery or selfishness in the framework of the Islamic government. Instead, there is legality and fulfilment of the lofty Shari'a of Muhammad, the peace and blessing of God be upon him, both in words and action. The Islamic state of Afghanistan, under the leadership of the Taliban Islamic movement, has put into practice everything that it has preached, according to God's law and the guidance of the magnificent Holy Qur'an. Any step which has been taken by the Islamic state has been in conformity with the Shari'a and whatever has been said in words has been implemented in action.

Thus the central tenet of the Taliban creed, when they took power in Kandahar in October 1994, was to free Afghanistan from the control of the Mujahidin parties that had run the government since April 1992 and to establish an Islamic state based on Shari'a law. They saw the ousted government as having failed to adhere to the standards expected of an Islamic state, in spite of the long involvement of its leaders in Islamist movements and the commitment of these leaders to the creation of such a state. Its replacement by a movement that was in a position to establish an Islamic government possessed of the necessary purity was therefore seen as justifiable.

Part of the international response to the Taliban's policies, both from the West and from other parts of the Islamic world, has been a reaction to their use of certain punishments laid down in Shari'a law, known as the Hudud. These include the stoning of adulterers and amputation for theft. There has been fierce debate between Islamic scholars throughout the history of Islam as to whether these forms of punishment should be applied and with what safeguards. Some countries, such as Saudi Arabia and the Sudan, use them. Others, such as Egypt, have resisted calls for their use. In justifying their use in Taliban-held areas of Afghanistan, Sher Muhammad Stanakzai, the acting foreign minister, speaking on Voice of Shari'a Radio, said, on 20 November:

> By the enforcement of Shari'a Hudud, we have made safe the lives and property of millions of people from Herat to Jalalabad and Kabul. No one can commit theft or crimes. We have not introduced this law. This is the law that was revealed by God to Muhammad. Those who consider the imposition of this law to be against human rights are insulting all Muslims and their beliefs.

The policies of the Taliban have also aroused controversy because of their particularly detailed and onerous restrictions on how women and men should dress and behave. On 6 December 1996, the Department for the Promotion of Virtue and Prevention of Vice announced that it had punished 225 women the previous day, in accordance with the Shari'a, for violating its rules on clothing. It stated:

> As the dignity and honour of a Muslim woman is ensured by observing *hejab* [seclusion from society] as requested by Shari'a, all honourable sisters are strongly asked to completely observe *hejab* as recommended by Shari'a. This can be achieved only if our dear sisters wear *burqas*, because full *hejab* cannot be achieved by wearing only a *chador* [a large piece of material that envelops the body and covers the head but leaves all or part of the face uncovered, at the discretion of the wearer]. In cases of violation, no one will have the right of complaint.

Men have also been required to conform to a strict dress code, avoiding Western clothing and abstaining from shaving. On 5 December 1996, the Department for the Promotion of Virtue and Prevention of Vice quoted a Hadith:

> Since the Prophet, Muhammad, peace be upon him, did not trim his beard all his life, therefore all government employees are hereby informed that they should grow their beards within a month and a half,

in accordance with the noble Hadith of the Prophet, in order to be regarded as a true Muslim.

The requirement that men should pray five times per day, ideally in a mosque, is consistent with the wish of the Taliban to ensure a higher degree of religious observance. Collective worship has traditionally been regarded as preferable to individual worship, even though individual worship has been widely practised. Bans on music, games and on the visual representation of the human or animal form also draw their inspiration from a conservative interpretation of the dictates of Islam.

The population of Kabul has perhaps been singled out as needing particular corrective action. The Taliban have their power base in the rural areas and in the more conservative south of Afghanistan and have viewed Kabul as a centre of liberalism, at best, and decadence, at worst. It is also seen as the source of both the socialist and Islamist movements which, they feel, have brought ruin on Afghanistan, and is believed to have been tainted by the secular attitudes brought in by Soviet advisers. Part of the Taliban's mission to cleanse is aimed at ensuring that the population of Kabul abandons all vestiges of alien cultures and ideologies. However, since the more liberal and affluent elements of Kabul society left during the period of Soviet occupation or following the establishment of the Mujahidin government, the Taliban are seeking to impose their vision on the relatively uneducated and impoverished population that remains. Mullah Omar clearly took account of this in a statement broadcast on Radio Voice of Shari'a on 5 December:

> A message of his eminence, Amir Al-Mu'minin, Mullah Muhammad Omar Mujahid, to office-holders and all other Taliban in Kabul. Create an atmosphere of security for the residents of Kabul who have suffered for several years. Refrain from any kind of ... violation. All your acts must be in line with the Shari'a so that you receive help from almighty God and the cooperation of the Muslim nation.

The Taliban's policies in Kabul and Herat are therefore very different from those in the rural areas, where the population have largely been left alone to live as they wished, with a minimum of interference. The urban areas have also been singled out because of fears that they might harbour sympathisers with the opposition forces. Efforts to disarm the population have consequently been particularly thorough, and there have been more arrests.

The military agenda, the objective of bringing the whole country under Taliban control, has been the most important one, followed closely by the imposition of prescribed codes of behaviour and dress. Every effort to raise the issue of female access to education and employment has thus been met with the response that this is a relatively low priority, and one that will have to await the successful conquest of Afghanistan.

It must be emphasised, however, that there are enormous differences within the ranks of the Taliban as regards gender and other issues, including the relationship with the West. There is the usual spectrum from hard-line to relatively moderate that is to be found in any radical movement. Although the movement has a high degree of cohesion in terms of its basic tenets, there are therefore inconsistencies in approach that render the process of interaction with the outside world particularly complex. The practice of moving Taliban officials fairly quickly from one posting to another, in order to prevent power bases being developed, has served to create confusion in the long-term planning of services to the population, as each will bring a different interpretation to the local situation.

The decision-making process within the Taliban leadership has also been somewhat unclear, particularly in the relationship between the Taliban in Kandahar and those in Kabul. The Taliban spokesman Mullah Wakil Ahmed, speaking to the Arabic magazine *Al-Majallah* on 23 October and responding to a question as to how decisions were taken within the Taliban movement, said:

> They are based on the advice of the Amir Al-Mu'minin. For us, consultation is not necessary. We believe that this is in line with the Sunnah. We abide by the Amir's view even if he alone takes this view ... There will not be a head of state. Instead, there will be an Amir Al-Mu'minin. Mullah Muhammad Omar will be the highest authority, and the government will not be able to implement any decision to which he does not agree ... General elections are incompatible with the Shari'a and therefore we reject them. Instead, we consult with eminent scholars who fulfil certain conditions.

Mullah Omar therefore has an important role as the symbolic leader of the movement as well as the ultimate decision-maker. However, it is clear that he draws heavily on the traditional consensual approach to decision-making in that the Kandahar *shura*, which brings together the leading figures within a governing council, operates very much by consensus. Similarly, the Taliban have explicitly endorsed the system of *jirgas*, made up of village elders and other notables, as the appropriate decision-making bodies at the village level, thus rejecting the participation on the basis of political party membership or military power that existed during the Soviet and Mujahidin period. The *jirgas*, which also rely on consensus, have re-established themselves with considerable effectiveness. Thus, while the Taliban might have a presence within a rural district, it is the *jirga* that has the determining role in matters of concern to the population. The Taliban also draw heavily on the views of the Ulema. It is thus the Ulema who will be called upon to consider how girls might best be educated to accord with the precepts of Islam, and it was the Ulema who were summoned by the Taliban leader after the events of September 11 2001 to pronounce on whether Osama bin Laden should be handed over to the USA.

One of the major difficulties in seeking to understand the belief system of the Taliban lies in assessing to what extent it draws on custom and practice within the Pushtun society of southern Afghanistan, as opposed to the various strands of thinking within the Indian subcontinent and the wider Islamic world. When asked what the differences were between the Afghan system and other systems, such as those in Iran, Sudan and others, Mullah Omar replied: 'We do not look at other governments. We do not have enough information on those states' systems.' This may well be the case, yet one has to take account of the fact that no entity is entirely impervious to the many influences that surround it. It is inevitable that the thinking of the Taliban will have, consciously or unconsciously, absorbed the various strands of thought that have characterised radical Islam over the past few decades. Thus, while recognising that one is being speculative, it is worth drawing parallels and comparisons with the other major movements of recent times, namely those of the Muslim Brotherhood, the Wahhabis, the Libyan Revolution and the Iranian revolution. These will be looked at in the next chapter.

6 Earlier Islamic Movements

There is a danger, in considering the various movements in the Islamic world, of attaching an easy label to them. The press has made frequent use of the term 'Islamic fundamentalist' as a catch-all phrase to cover any movement that has taken even a remotely radical form. Certainly, much has been written about the growth of both Islamic and Christian fundamentalist movements in response to particular societal crises. However, the term 'Islamic fundamentalism' is often used in a pejorative sense. Examples of excesses by radical groups throughout the world are used, implicitly, to brand all Muslims as extremists.

It is important not to fall into the trap of labelling the Taliban, not least because it can be regarded as drawing on quite a number of influences. This chapter instead seeks to explore the possible origins of the Taliban creed and so to highlight the complexities of the movement rather than over-simplify it. It focuses first on parallels with the movements that took root in Egypt, Saudi Arabia, Libya and Iran during the twentieth century.

As indicated in Chapter 5, a major element of the debate within the Islamic world over the past century or so has been how far Islam should adapt itself to the dominant Western cultures. Governments in Islamic countries have found themselves under increasing attack from radical movements within their own borders for being too accommodating with the West. Such movements have found favour with the most impoverished sections of society, acutely conscious of their lack of access to the riches enjoyed by privileged elites within their own countries and of the affluent lifestyles of Westerners. Radical Islam has thus been a response to relative disadvantage as well as to the chaos of civil conflict.

One such movement, and one that has been enormously influential, is the Muslim Brotherhood. It was created in Egypt in 1928, originally as a youth movement, and set out to counter the influence among young people of the secular and liberal ideas gaining ground at the time, with Marxism singled out as being of particular concern. Brotherhood leaders were also outraged at the level of injustice and decadence they perceived in Egypt. The Brotherhood quickly developed into a mass movement, building up a network of branches, each with its own centre, incorporating a mosque, a school and other facilities. The schools provided religious and physical education, including military training, to prepare the students for a jihad, aimed at liberating Egypt from British control and protecting the 'Islamic homeland' from Western influences.

An important part of the Brotherhood's appeal has been its strong commitment to social justice, given concrete form through the organisation of social assistance programmes in both villages and urban neighbourhoods. It is also significant in asserting that Islam could legitimately encompass every aspect of the political, economic, social and cultural life of the believer. In 1929, the Brotherhood stated:

a) Islam is a comprehensive self-evolving system; it is the ultimate path of life in all its spheres.
b) Islam emanates from, and is based on, two fundamental sources: the Qur'an and the Prophetic tradition.
c) Islam is applicable to all times and places.

It further stated that the 'Islamic homeland' was to benefit from a 'free Islamic government, practising the principles of Islam, applying its social system, propounding its solid fundamentals and transmitting its wise call to the people'. The movement adopted the slogan: 'The Qur'an is our constitution. The Prophet is our Guide; Death for the glory of Allah is our greatest ambition.'

One of the leading ideologues of the Muslim Brotherhood, Muhammad Ghazali, in his book *Our Beginning in Wisdom*, published in 1948, argued that the Shari'a had to be the source of law in all aspects of life – social, political or economic. Another ideologue, Sayyid Qutb, writing in the early 1950s, took their thinking further in promoting the concept of pan-Islam, of an international community of believers (*umma*) in which national boundaries were of no consequence. During his trial in 1965, on a charge of sedition that led to his execution by the Egyptian government of Gamal Abdul Nasser, he argued: 'The bonds of ideology and belief are sturdier than those of patriotism, based on region, and this false distinction among Muslims on a regional basis is but one expression of crusading and Zionist imperialism that must be eradicated.'

Sayyid Qutb also put forward the important principle that Islam gave Muslims the right to attack a person or his property if, by his actions, they considered that he did not merit being regarded as a believer. This notion justified the use of jihad to oppose those in power. The assassination of Egyptian President Anwar Sadat in 1981 was a direct consequence of this ideological position. The organisation that carried it out, Munazzamat Al-Jihad, justified the killing on the grounds that Sadat had made peace with Israel, and that the current laws of Egypt, being incompatible with the Shari'a, imposed suffering on believing Muslims. Prior to the assassination, Al-Jihad's leader issued a fatwa that declared Sadat to be an unbeliever and thus legitimised the action. The ideological underpinning of Al-Jihad's act, drafted by Muhammad Abdul Salam Faraj, held that every true Muslim is obliged by his faith to struggle for the revival of the Islamic *umma* and that Muslim groups or leaders who have turned away from the Shari'a are apostates. Armed struggle was seen as the only acceptable form of jihad. The internal unbeliever had first to be confronted, and then the external ones. Leadership of the Islamic *umma* had to be given to the strongest among the believers who also feared Allah. He had to be chosen collectively and then obeyed.

One can see a number of parallels here with the creed of the Taliban. One is the very clear implication from their statements and actions that Islam is not simply a basis for individual faith but a system that encompasses all aspects of society, including individual behaviour and the relationship of the individual to both society and state. There is therefore no question of the state being a secular entity and of religion being relegated to the private sphere. The state is seen as the collective embodiment of the Islamic values espoused by society, and its continued existence is dependent on the commitment of citizens to uphold and defend these values.

Another important parallel is the right of a movement to take up arms against an existing Islamic government that is considered as insufficiently pure in its adherence to Islam. The assassination of Anwar Sadat, a committed Muslim, on the grounds that, through his actions, he had acted against what were interpreted as the interests of Muslims, provides a clear precedent for the overthrow, through a jihad, of a government that claims to be Islamic but is regarded as having contravened Islamic values. Thus, while Rabbani, Masoud and Hekmatyar had led Islamist parties and Rabbani had been a lecturer in Islamic theology, their failure to create a united Islamic government was felt to justify military action against them. The assassination of Najibullah, who, although he asserted his allegiance to Islam, was identified with the secular values of the Soviet Union, is not necessarily consistent with this principle.

The exclusive reliance on Shari'a law is a further significant element in the positive comparisons that can be drawn with the Muslim Brotherhood. While the Taliban's interpretation of Shari'a law may be quite different from that of the Brotherhood, the fact that it is regarded as the legal code to guide the actions of both the state and the individual is a clear parallel.

The emphasis in the ideology of the Brotherhood and in the Taliban creed on the need to choose a leader collectively and then obey him is also of interest. One is immediately struck by the similar process in the Catholic Church, with the Pope being elected by the College of Cardinals and then being accorded infallibility. There is certainly an aura of infallibility around Mullah Omar, even though he is accountable to the governing *shura*, which is in many respects comparable to the College of Cardinals in incorporating religious scholars.

It is less easy to determine whether the young followers of the Taliban have the same motivation as the youth who joined the Muslim Brotherhood. While the footsoldiers of the Taliban have been relatively uneducated, the question of disadvantage is much less of a factor than the response to the conflict. However, it could be argued that the Taliban recruits who have come from the refugee camps in Pakistan have been exposed to the relative affluence of the West, both through contact with aid organisations and through the television screens they may have seen when visiting nearby cities. They would also have been aware of the corruption involved in the distribution of food rations in the camps. They would have been provided with military training by the Mujahidin parties present in the camps, together with the basic Islamic education given in the camp *madrasahs*. Some will already have had experience of fighting for one or other of the Mujahidin parties. Years in the refugee camps will have created a loose sense of identity and a consequent vulnerability to a movement that offers certainties and a clear way forward.

As already mentioned, there was no concept of pan-Islam in the Taliban creed when they first came to power. If anything, there was competition with other Islamic movements on the basis of relative purity. There was also a strongly nationalistic element in their approach. There was an absolute focus on the need to take control of the geographical entity known as Afghanistan and a clearly stated denial to fears from the north that they would seek to spread their creed to the Muslims of Central Asia. It was almost as if, in their fixation on the conquest or, in their terms, liberation of Afghanistan, there was a wish to treat a sick patient, a victim of aggression and civil conflict, who was in danger of rapidly deteriorating if radical action was not taken. The remedy, in this case, was Islam. However, the US air strikes of August 1998 imposed a pan-Islamic mantle upon them as they became labelled by virtue of their association with Osama bin Laden. It is interesting that the Taliban leader spoke of the need to address the issues of Palestine and the US military presence in Saudi Arabia following the attacks on the World Trade Center and the Pentagon in September 2001.

The Wahhabi movement in Saudi Arabia has also possibly influenced the Taliban. Its founder, Muhammad Ibn Abdul Wahhab (1703–87), was concerned at the superstition prevalent in Arabian, society, and at the lax observance of Islamic rites and practices. He called for a discarding of all medieval superstitions and for the exercise of *ijtihad* (the right to reinterpret Islam based on changing conditions). His followers armed themselves and launched a jihad against those they deemed guilty of idolatry, injustice, corruption and adultery, regarding themselves to be the true believers. They also imposed an unprecedented degree of puritanism on the community, banning music, dancing, poetry and the use of silk, gold, ornaments or jewellery. The Wahhabis seized Mecca in 1803 and were able to hold on to it until they were defeated by the Ottomans in 1819.

The Wahhabi ideology was adopted by Abdul Aziz ibn Abdul Rahman Al-Saud, a descendant of the early Wahhabi leaders, in the early part of the twentieth century. He sought to transform the nomadic tribes inhabiting central Arabia, who had reverted to the use of tribal law and practised pre-Islamic rituals, into a unified Islamic *umma* by replacing loyalty to the tribe with loyalty to Islam and to its leader, the Imam. Abdul Aziz emphasised the socio-religious equality of all believers and thereby won support from the lower tribes of this highly hierarchical society. Taking on the identity of the 'truly guided Islamic community', the Wahhabis set out to attack those who claimed to be Muslim but whose behaviour was, in their view, un-Islamic. They took a hard line in defining who could be regarded as a believer, stating that no deviation from the Shari'a was permitted and that any Muslim who disagreed with the Wahhabi interpretation of Islam deserved severe punishment. The Wahhabis drew a firm distinction between the world of believers and that of unbelievers.

Abdul Aziz set up colonies of his followers, who were known as Ikhwan (brothers). These became the religious, political, military, administrative and educational centres of Wahhabism and made it possible for Abdul Aziz to exercise control over all the tribes of central Arabia. An important role in the colonies was played by the Ulema and by the religious police, who enforced compliance with the restrictions on music, dancing and so on and punished those failing to observe the Islamic rituals. Committees for the Promotion of Virtue and Prevention of Vice were set up to oversee the process of enforcement.

Like the early followers of Muhammad in the seventh century, the Wahhabis began a crusade to spread their beliefs throughout the Arabian peninsula and beyond. The colonies provided a ready source of recruits and the fighters showed themselves willing to martyr themselves for the cause. In the early 1920s, Abdul Aziz conquered one area of Arabia after another. He presented every campaign as a struggle to punish either religious dissenters or those who had strayed from true Islam.

In 1924 Abdul Aziz conquered Mecca, having previously condemned its leader for the corrupt way in which he managed Mecca and Medina, and called upon the Ikhwan to overthrow him. However, compromises subsequently made with the people of the city, after his assumption of control, alienated the 150,000 men living in the Ikhwan colonies. While he was seeking international recognition in relation to the 80 per cent of Arabia he had conquered, his forces continued to engage in warfare beyond these boundaries and he was finally compelled to seek help from Britain to bring these forces under control. Abdul Aziz proclaimed himself king of Saudi Arabia in 1932 and established a dynasty, legitimised by Islam, that has continued up to the present time.

One can see many similarities between the Taliban and the Wahhabi movement. Both mobilised men to martyr themselves with the aim of conquering a country, overthrowing a government regarded as un-Islamic and establishing an Islamic state. Both also insisted that their interpretation (*ijtihad*) of Islam was the only correct one. The right of *ijtihad* asserted by the Wahhabis appears to be an inherent element in the Taliban creed. In their rejection of criticisms levelled by the Islamic government of Iran, among others, that their belief system is not consistent with Islam, they have insisted that their interpretation of Islam has a greater validity and purity than that of the Iranian government. There is therefore an implicit assumption that Islam is not susceptible to a common interpretation throughout the Islamic world but may be continually reinterpreted by those seeking to purify it.

The extreme puritanism apparent in the Wahhabi ideology, manifested in the prohibitions on music and dancing and in the enforcement of religious observance, is also present in the Taliban. The establishment by the Taliban of a Department for the Promotion of Virtue and Prevention of Vice, and the strong emphasis on the enforcement of regulations, are directly derived from Wahhabism. The pronounced focus on the eradication of corruption as both a justification for a jihad and as an objective is a further similarity. However, the Taliban appear to be rather more ardent in their attacks on corruption than, on the face of it, the Wahhabis.

In looking at the military and political strategies of the Taliban, one could speculate that they may be mindful of the split that eventually occurred between Abdul Aziz and his followers and of his consequent need to seek the support of the West to bring them under control. The Taliban are clearly extremely concerned not to weaken the resolve of their footsoldiers, on whom they depend to achieve their ambition of bringing Afghanistan under their control. They evidently fear that any modification of their policies in response to Western pressures will provoke accusations from their followers that they are no longer acting in accordance with the jihad for which men have martyred themselves.

The wish of the Taliban to protect Afghanistan from non-Islamic elements produces echoes of Moamar al Gaddafi, who took power in Libya in 1969 and created an ideology that had the eradication of Western influence at its core. The slogan of the Libyan revolution was 'Freedom, Socialism and Unity'. 'Freedom' denoted freedom from Western economic, political and cultural domination, and manifested itself in the nationalisation of foreign assets and in the eradication of cultural influences such as Western music and night-clubs. 'Socialism' was seen as a combination of state control of the economy and a generous system of health and welfare provision. 'Unity' referred to the unity of the Arab world within the unity of the Islamic world within the unity of the Third World, all in opposition to the West.

While the Taliban are clearly seeking to free Afghanistan of outside influences, nothing that they have said to date indicates that they regard socialism as anything but the alien ideology the Soviet Union sought to introduce into Afghanistan, or that they see social justice as more than the exercise of Islamic charity by the population through the *zakat* or tythe system. However, they do now appear to feel some sense of solidarity with other parts of the Islamic world, particularly in the wake of the US air strikes on Afghanistan of August 1998 and the events of September 2001.

There are comparable similarities with the Iranian revolution of 1979, which set out to create a society in which Western economic, political, cultural and religious influences were minimised and in which a highly organised structure of government ensured that Islamic principles underpinned all aspects of life. This includes a strong emphasis on social justice, manifested in, for example, priority being given to health and education programmes and to the provision of subsidies on basic essentials.

Among the factors leading to the revolution in Iran were attempts by the Shah to challenge existing interpretations of Shari'a law. These met with fierce resistance from the Ulema and led to massive street demonstrations, which were brutally repressed. Some of the Ulema then called for a jihad against what they regarded as the un-Islamic government of the Shah.

The leading ideologue of the Iranian revolution was Ayatollah Ruhollah Khomeini. He argued that the Ulema should commit them-

selves to ousting corrupt officials and to replacing them with regimes
led by Islamic jurists, and urged them to build a mass movement. He
proposed that political power should be subordinated to Islamic precepts, criteria and objectives and that the Ulema should participate in
its legislative, executive and judicial organs. He insisted that an Islamic
state should have an Islamic ruler, a religious jurist with a full knowledge of Shari'a law. The leader would be assisted by jurisprudents at
various levels of legislative, executive and judicial bodies. A popularly
elected parliament would resolve the conflicts that were likely to arise
in the implementation of Islamic doctrines, and the administration
would be carried out by civil servants who were familiar with the law
relating to their functions. However, only jurisprudents would be involved in the judicial process, and they would also oversee the legislative
and executive aspects of the state. A key aspect of Khomeini's policy
was his fierce determination that Iran should not be dependent on
foreign powers, and the USA was identified as the major threat to
Iran's independence.

In building up his movement before the overthrow of the Shah,
Khomeini attached symbolic importance to the mosque as an institu-
tion central to the Islamic society he was aiming to create, and used the
mosque as the base for a network of revolutionary committees.

The Iranian revolution demonstrates parallels with the Taliban
movement in so far as both set out to generate a mass following of
people who were divorced from the relatively powerful and wealthy
elites who exercised control. In Iran, the contrast between the affluent
and Westernised middle classes and the urban and rural poor was very
stark. In Afghanistan, there was concern that some of the Mujahidin
parties were rumoured to be receiving large amounts of money from
external backers and from involvement in the black economy. Both
presented Islam as an all-encompassing religion and argued that an
Islamic state should embrace the social, economic, political and judicial
spheres. There is also apparent in the Iranian revolution and in the
Taliban movement, as with the Muslim Brotherhood, a significant level
of participation by young people, with the result that these movements
have benefited from the radicalism, passion and uncompromising purity
characteristic of certain strands of youth.

One can also see a link between the emphasis on the religious leader in Iran, with his reliance on Islamic scholars for advice, and the designation of Mullah Omar as Amir Al-Mu'minin and his dependence on the Ulema – for example, in drawing up an education curriculum. Mullah Omar's very simple lifestyle resembles that of the Ayatollah Khomeini in Iran. The major difference between the two men is that Mullah Omar, although he has studied the Qur'an, is not a scholar in the sense that Khomeini was, nor does he claim to be. He therefore looks to the Ulema for guidance on Shari'a law.

A further similarity between the Iranian revolution and the Taliban movement is the emphasis on the mosque. Although the Taliban have given no indication that they plan to set up revolutionary committees, their insistence that men pray in the mosque rather than separately may be aimed to create a strong sense of cohesion within the Islamic state that they wish to establish.

An apparent difference between the two movements is in the degree of prior planning for the exercise of government. Ayatollah Khomeini, before taking power, had drawn up a highly detailed blueprint of how the state should be structured and organised. The Taliban, by contrast, happened upon power almost by accident and, although they may have received a great deal of prior and subsequent advice by their backers regarding the organisation of government, this appears to have focused largely on military strategy and the maintenance of law and order. There have been a number of statements as to how the administration of government might be improved but this has, so far, been given little priority. There has also been little apparent consideration as to how best to persuade the population of the Taliban creed, whereas in Iran the process of ideological promotion is highly sophisticated. The Taliban instead rely partly on a reinforcement of traditional beliefs and structures and partly on the use of force and fear to impose their creed. These methods are of course used in Iran, but it also makes effective use of the media, of specially created structures and of the education system to promote the ideology espoused by the state.

In summarising, it would be unwise to state that the Taliban have drawn their inspiration from any particular movement. However, its members have been brought up and educated in an environment in which many of these ideas have been in circulation. One can also see very obvious influences – the Department for the Promotion of Virtue and the Prevention of Vice, for instance, is modelled on those of the Wahhabi movement. Thus one should not discount the influence of other Islamic movements even if the Taliban give the appearence, at least, of drawing heavily on Afghan custom and practice in relation to Islam.

7 The Afghan Islamic tradition

As in other parts of the world, popular belief in Afghanistan has been based on a mixture of superstition, spiritualism, saint worship, mysticism and organised religion. Islam has therefore been mixed with pre-Islamic beliefs and with tribal codes such as the Pushtunwali.

Belief in Islam has, however, been important for the population, not only in providing spiritual fulfilment but also in giving a sense of identity to the people of the area. In fact it could be said that, before the beginning of the twentieth century, the people of what is now Afghanistan saw themselves as part of a Sunni Muslim entity, sandwiched between the two infidel empires of Britain and Russia and Shi'a Iran, rather than as citizens of a nation. The self-identification of the population as being primarily Muslim therefore has strong roots. They have been relatively relaxed in their adherence to ritual observances, and relatively unpuritanical in their appreciation of art, music and poetry. Yet Afghanistan has always been a highly conservative society. Even in Kabul, which has been more liberal than the rural areas, society has been dominated by convention and Islam has had a strong hold.

Islam has been particularly sensitive to outside influences. As it spread eastward, it had to contend with Hinduism and Buddhism and scholars had to decide whether to adapt Islam to these other religions or to seek a return to a purer form of Islam through the eradication of the Hindu and Buddhist influences that had crept in. There were Islamic revivalist movements from the sixteenth century onwards, centred on the mystic Sufi scholars of the Naqshandi order.

The presence of British India and its dominant role in the region brought Western influences to the very border of what is now Afghanistan. Islam became the rallying cry of many resistance movements, and the Pushtun tribes of the north-west frontier region provided ready recruits. A key role was played in this process by Sayyad Ahmed Barelvi (1786–1831), who came from north-east India. He built up a movement by travelling throughout the Indian subcontinent, and identified the North-West Frontier Province as a base from which to attack the British. He drew on the Ulema as the power base of the movement, ignoring the tribal leaders, and called on the people to undertake a jihad against the British. Barelvi demanded that the Shari'a replace tribal law. The term *jamaat*, or society, was used to describe the movement, which can thus be seen as an early example of a political party based on Islam. Survivors of the movement took part in a major rebellion against the British in India in 1857.

From this arose an initiative to create a School of Islamic Studies at Deoband, near Delhi, in 1867, at which several generations of Afghan Ulema came to be trained. The Ulema had studied the Qur'an, the Hadith and Islamic law, and were thus in a position to advise on behaviour consistent with Islam. It was they who dispensed justice and they would normally meet collectively in a council, or *shura*, when there were important matters to discuss. During the 1930s and 1940s, when the power of the Ulema was at its greatest, they advised the legislative and executive branches of the government on religious matters. They had control of the courts and schools and also had an oversight on public and private morality and customs. At this time, they were paid by the government. The Ulema were distinct from the mullahs, who had received a basic training in the main elements of Islam, sufficient to enable them to lead prayers at the local mosque and to provide some guidance on Islamic observance. Ulema tended to be dismissive of practices such as the worship of saints, whereas mullahs would normally participate fully in them.

The Deoband school drew heavily on the Sufi tradition of Afghanistan and was highly orthodox in its interpretation of Islam. There was a clear emphasis on pan-Islam as a means of overriding ethnic, linguistic, tribal and other loyalties. The need to engage in a jihad against the British in India was an important element.

Former pupils of Deoband continued to encourage the tribes of the north-west frontier to take up arms against the British. They were instrumental in establishing a chain of Islamic schools, or *madrasahs*, along the frontier, which have provided many of the Afghan Ulema since 1947. From the 1950s onwards, additional *madrasahs* were set up by the Islamist parties and by the Wahhabis.

The abortive attempts of Britain to take Afghanistan during the nineteenth century and the pressure from the north, first from Russia and then from the Soviet Union, have strengthened the resolve of the Ulema to resist outside interference and to render the government of Afghanistan more purely Islamic. There has also been a resistance to the state by much of the population, particularly those in the rural areas. The state first emerged as a mechanism through which the dominant Pushtun tribe, which had conquered large areas of what is now Afghanistan, could consolidate its hold. Shari'a law was seen by the Afghan monarchy in the nineteenth century as a useful basis for cementing the society into a governable unit. However, tribal and village communities consistently held out against any intrusion by state officials.

Amir Abdur-Rahman introduced piecemeal changes to the administration during his reign (1880–1901) in order to increase its effectiveness, but did not set out to challenge the existing thinking of the population. However, King Amanullah, who reigned from 1919 to 1929, sought to impose modernity on Afghanistan as a means of strengthening its capacity to withstand non-Islamic influences – in his perception Afghanistan was vulnerable because it was backward. Amanullah placed a strong emphasis on education, in an effort to introduce Western concepts into the national psyche and to counter what he saw as outmoded ideas. As a result, education came to be viewed as an attempt to reduce the influence of Islam. His reforms, which bore the trappings of Western culture and were seen as autocratically presented, seriously offended the traditional leadership and the Ulema.

In January 1929 the opposition forces gathered behind Habibullah II, a Tajik who had the active support of the Ulema. In laying siege to Kabul from the north, he demanded that Amanullah reverse his reforms. Amanullah accepted but was overthrown a few days later by Bacha-e-Saqqao. The latter promised to establish Shari'a law, dissolved the Education and Justice Ministries and gave responsibility for the education and legal systems to the Ulema.

However, he failed to maintain his position and was replaced by Muhammad Nadir Khan, a third cousin of Amanullah, in October 1929. The reasons for his overthrow are of interest in relation to the present situation. The tribal leadership of the Pushtuns, although they had an ambivalent relationship with the Ulema, could not tolerate the idea of a Tajik ruling over them. They therefore came to an arrangement with the Ulema whereby they shifted their support from Habibullah II to a new leader designated by the Pushtun tribes without modifying the objective of creating an Islamic state based on Shari'a law. The Ulema thus had a significant influence over the new king, and a structure was created through which all laws and regulations were vetted by a body of Ulema to ensure their consistency with Shari'a law.

When Nadir Khan was assassinated in November 1933 and his son, Zahir Shah, became king, the religious establishment remained powerful. In 1944 a School for Instruction in the Shari'a was set up, which developed into the Faculty of Theology at Kabul University in 1950. Previously, Ulema had been trained at Deoband or Al-Azhar in Cairo. It now became possible for them to receive training in Afghanistan.

Many of the religious leaders at that time were influenced by the thinking of the Pakistani Islamic theorist Abdul Ala Maududi, who in 1941 had established the Jamaat-e-Islami party in India, which became Pakistan's Jamaat-e-Islami party in 1947. He was highly elitist in his approach in that he set out to influence those holding power in society as a means of promoting change within it. This was quite distinct from the policy of the Muslim Brotherhood, which advocated the building of change from the bottom, through the development of mass movements. He described the West as morally decadent and corrupt and argued that Islam was self-sufficient and quite separate from, and indeed opposed to, both Western and socialist ways of life. He advocated total reliance on the Shari'a, while recognising the need for interpretation in response to changing circumstances.

Maududi's influence can clearly be seen in much of what the Taliban stand for. Their conviction that there should be no compromise with Western values and that, instead, the West should respect and accommodate itself to the value system espoused by the Taliban movement is an obvious parallel. The total reliance on the Shari'a, and the assertion by the Taliban that they have the right to interpret Islam anew and that theirs is the correct interpretation, also carry echoes of Maududi. As indicated in the next chapter, Maududi's ultra-conservative view on the seclusion of women provided ideological justification for the position taken by the Taliban.

The Soviet invasion provided the opportunity for the Islamist movement, much weakened by recent purges, to strengthen its ranks. Islam therefore became the binding force of the resistance movement and a jihad was called against the invaders, whence the resistance fighters took on the name of the Mujahidin. As noted earlier, the seven Mujahidin parties supported by Pakistan, the USA and Saudi Arabia were composed of two primary elements: the Islamist parties, led by intellectuals, who had borrowed Western political concepts in order to create a new political ideology based on a reinterpretation of the Qur'an and the Hadith, and the so-called traditionalists, who drew their support from the Ulema, the mullahs, and tribal and other leaders. They based their interpretation of Islam on a long history of scholastic commentary on the Qur'an and also drew on other traditions, including those relating to the behaviour of women.

However, there was a spectrum within each of the two camps. Within the Islamist camp, at one end was Hisb-e-Islami (Hekmatyar), which sought a radical restructuring of society. It took the view that the dominance of society by the Ulema and the consequent reliance on legal tradition was archaic and inappropriate to a modern society. In its place it created a political ideology that drew on a re-reading of the Qur'an and the Hadith but disregarded the complex body of law that had been built up over the centuries. Hisb-e-Islami also opted to disseminate its ideology by creating a party structure very much modelled on that of the Soviet Communist Party and of revolutionary movements in other parts of the world. By establishing a network of cells, made up of well-trained adherents, it was hoped that a movement could gradually be built up that could take power and create an Islamic state. The same organisational structure would then work to build adherence to the ideology within the wider population and so replace the existing beliefs, structures and relationships.

At the other end of the spectrum among the Islamists were Jamiat-i-Islami and Hisb-e-Islami (Khalis), with broadly similar objectives to those of Hisb-e-Islami but quite different views as to how these objectives should be achieved. They were thus agreed on the ultimate aim of creating an Islamic state that had its foundation in a new political ideology, drawing on the essential elements of Islam, rather than the legalistic tradition of the Ulema. However, they felt that it was necessary to bring the Ulema on board and to build support within their ranks and within the ranks of tribal leaders in order to change both society and the relationship between society and state.

Within the ranks of the so-called traditionalist parties there was a clear spectrum from Mujadidi, who had shown definite sympathies for an Islamist approach over his life but was none the less firmly rooted in tradition, through to the liberalism of Gailani, with Harakat, in between, representing the Ulema and tribal elders. These were also not parties in the strict sense of the meaning, but simply called themselves parties in order to gain access to the resources provided by the three backers of the Mujahidin.

In the event, the Islamist parties, collectively, did adopt an approach that respected the roles and perspectives of the Ulema and also the consensual decision-making processes of traditional society. Olivier Roy thus notes the political programme of the Islamist parties:

> Sovereignty belongs to God alone. The Amir is only a representative and the only source of true authority is religious. The Amir is selected by a consensus of the whole community, expressed concretely by election ... The powers of the Amir are considerable but he is assisted by a Shura or council. The body of the Ulema retains its autonomy with regard to the political power and may censure or depose an Amir. Civil society is under the control of the Ulema acting within the limits of the Shari'a (Roy, 1986: 82).

The major Shi'a party, Hisb-e-Wahdat, perhaps went further than this approach in establishing what was clearly an Islamist regime within the Hazarajat, modelled on the thinking of Ayatollah Khomeini. However, while the decison-making process at the district level was based on a cell structure, at the village level the old consensual tradition continued to exist.

The war brought other religious influences into Afghanistan. The Afghan jihad took on an enormous symbolic importance for adherents to radical Islam throughout the Islamic world, and attracted large numbers of volunteers from the Middle East and elsewhere to fight alongside the Mujahidin. Many of these received military training for the first time during their participation in the jihad. Some went on to fight in Bosnia or to organise movements in their countries of origin, using terrorist tactics, among others, to the considerable concern of many Arab and other governments of Muslim countries.

There has been considerable ambivalence within both Afghanistan and Pakistan to the Arab presence and to the presence of other Muslims. This ambivalence has been felt more acutely in the tribal areas, where resistance to foreign interference has traditionally been stronger, than in the north of Afghanistan, including the Shomali area to the north of Kabul, where radicalism has more easily taken hold. Kunduz has been a particular base for Muslim volunteers, many of whom fought in the incursionary movement against the Tajik government from 1993 to 1997 and subsequently lent support to the Taliban. Since the US air strikes of 1998, the opposition forces have, in their statements, made it clear that they regard the volunteers from other parts of the world as being party to an attempt by Pakistan to colonise Afghanistan.

The Wahhabi movement has also had a significant influence, particularly in Kunar, but it is important to note that such influence was already felt before the PDPA coup. There was, therefore, a receptivity within the province to the extreme radicalism and puritanism of this particular ideology.

The war provided the opportunity for a new generation of adherents to radical Islam, or to Islamist ideologies, to be trained. Saudi Arabia was extremely active in developing universities, *madrasahs* and mosques in Afghanistan and in the Afghan refugee camps in Pakistan. Hisb-e-Islami (Hekmatyar) had its own educational institutions and its own camps. The radical parties in Pakistan also played a role in promoting their particular approaches to Islam. Orphanages were an important mechanism for influencing young people, and the poverty of many families led them to take advantage of the board and lodging and additional allowances provided by the various parties and movements that operated these orphanages. It is quite possible, therefore, that a proportion of the young people who have joined the Taliban were schooled in the educational establishments set up by the Islamist parties. However, there is a clear difference between the position of the Islamists and that of the Taliban.

The Taliban can be seen as distinct from the Islamist Mujahidin parties in that they are not seeking to create a political ideology. Rather, using Shari'a law as their sole guide to action in governing the country, they are looking to the Ulema to provide guidance as to how they should proceed in any given situation. To a significant degree, one can therefore say that they are seeking a return to the situation that existed before Daoud began his reform programme in the late 1950s, when the Ulema held sway following the abortive overtures to modernity introduced by King Amanullah. As indicated earlier, its creed approximates most to that of the Harakat party within the Mujahidin. It has, however, inevitably been influenced by the policies of the Islamist parties, as these were influenced before the Soviet invasion by the views of the Ulema and the mullahs. For example, the system proposed by the Islamist parties, noted in the quotation by Oliver Roy above, very much corresponds to that established by the Taliban.

However, the Taliban have been stricter than the Mujahidin parties in many respects. Thus, while the Mujahidin leaders were always careful not to offend the Ulema and the mullahs, they were less severe in their enforcement of, for example, codes of dress or restrictions on the playing of music. They were also apparently unconcerned at the representation of the human or animal form, although its prohibition is consistent with conservative Muslim thinking.

Also significant is the influence on the Taliban of Pushtunwali (the traditional code of conduct in the Pushtun area, which could also be said to constitute a creed). This, for example, demands blood vengeance, even on fellow Muslims. It contradicts the Sura in the Qur'an that says: 'It is not for a believer to kill a believer unless it be by mistake', and enjoins that blood money be paid to the victim's family. Pushtunwali also includes a strong focus on hospitality, bravery, chivalry and the defence of honour, particularly that of women.

Pushtunwali and Shari'a law are at variance on some matters. For example, proof of adultery in Shari'a law is dependent on the evidence of four witnesses. In Pushtunwali, hearsay evidence is sufficient because it is the honour of the family that is the issue, not the morality of the situation. Women in Pushtun society are not allowed to inherit property, whereas the Qur'an provides that the woman shall inherit half the share of the male.

There has historically been a tension between Pushtunwali and Islam, with Islam – and the Ulema, who are the main vehicles for its promotion – representing a movement away from inward-looking tribalism towards a transcendence over tribal, ethnic and national allegiances. This has manifested itself in struggles for influence and power between Ulema and tribal leaders, the latter backed by mullahs. Periodically, the Ulema have called on men in the tribal areas to fight in a jihad, and this has been done without regard to the views or authority of the tribal leaders.

An important element in Pushtun culture is that the adherents to Pushtunwali attach greater importance to the value system it incorporates than to their membership of the Pushtun community or of the nation. One can see here a possible parallel with the Taliban emphasis on values and the very clear view that the preservation and promotion of these values take precedence over material considerations.

It is tempting to suggest that, because the Taliban originated in the Pushtun heartland, their philosophy owes much to Pushtunwali. In fact it could be said that it comes from the tradition whereby the Ulema used to call on men to disregard Pushtunwali for a period in favour of the Shari'a in order to engage in a jihad against a common enemy. However, it is interesting that the Taliban originated in the Pushtun tribal areas rather than the north, where the religious tradition was very different and, perhaps, more open to Islamist ideologies than the impassioned response to a call to jihad in defence of traditional values present in the south. It is also of note that Mullah Omar was a member of the Hisb-e-Islami (Khalis) party which, of the seven Mujahidin parties, most reflected the values of the Ulema and the tribal leaders. We may therefore be seeing a re-run of the 1929 overthrow of the Tajik ruler Bacha-e-Saqqao by the traditional Pushtun leaders in the ousting, by the Taliban, of the Tajik President Rabbani and the northern Pushtun Gulbuddin Hekmatyar, both of whom are Islamists.

To summarise, one can see a range of influences in the creed of the Taliban, drawn from Islamic movements in the Middle East, Iran, the Indian subcontinent and Afghanistan. However, the dominant influence appears to be that of the Afghan Ulema, who could be perceived as seeking a return to the status quo that existed before the intellectual movements of the 1950s and 1960s set in motion a chain of events from which Afghanistan is still reeling.

8 The Gender Policies of the Taliban

> Women ... are not just the biological reproducers of the nation, but also its cultural reproducers, often being given the task of guardians of 'culture' who are responsible for transmitting it to the children and constructing the 'home' in a specific cultural style. (Nira Yuval-Davis, 1997: 116).

In Afghanistan the process of achieving equal rights for women has not been an easy one. In fact for much of the population, living in the rural areas, the question of female employment and education has not been an issue. Women have always worked on the land and have been provided with a minimal level of education consistent with this role and with their role as parents. In the urban areas, even up to the late twentieth century, it has been the tradition that girls receive a reasonable level of education but that women, once married, do not work unless they have to. As women gradually entered the workforce in Kabul from the 1950s, they went into the usual service roles: secretaries, nurses, receptionists, air hostesses. A minority studied for the professions and became doctors, lawyers, engineers and journalists. Yet the traditional leaders and Ulema put considerable energy into opposing even this slow pace of change. At the root of their conservatism was a fear that, if women were educated or worked, they would be influenced by Western and secular ideas and would instil these into their children.

However one defines the Taliban creed, they are clearly at the conservative end of the spectrum. There are four main elements to their policy: a ban on the employment of women, except in the health sector; a temporary halt to formal female education pending the drawing up of an appropriate curriculum; the imposition of strict dress codes on both women and men requiring women to wear *burqas* and men to wear beards, unstyled hair, turbans and *shalwar kameez*; and the introduction of strict controls on the movement of women outside the home so that women are always separated from male strangers or are escorted by male relatives. The Taliban have stated that they will consider allowing women to work once they have made arrangements allowing women and men to work separately and travel separately.

However, elements within the Taliban have permitted humanitarian agencies to employ women in particular roles, where access to women is needed or where women work separately from men, under the direction of other women. It is not clear whether the authority thus given is sanctioned by the Taliban movement as a whole, and there have been oscillating responses to it by the Department for the Promotion of Virtue and the Prevention of Vice. The greatest impact of the ban on female employment has been on the education sector. Boys' schools, as well as girls' schools, have had to close because women are no longer allowed to work as teachers.

Another major impact has been on the number of children working in the streets. Women who were previously in employment or who survived through small trade have lost a crucial source of income. In spite of the extended family system this will have seriously affected the ability of many families to survive economically; families exclusively dependent on female earnings, and without extended family support, have been reduced to the margins. A significant number have had no choice but to ask their children to sell odd bits of things on the street or to beg for food or money. Many of the 50,000 refugees who fled to Pakistan in the months following the Taliban takeover of Kabul did so because they were suddenly deprived of female earnings.

Similarly, although the Taliban have had, at times, strong support among the refugee population in Pakistan, many refugees have felt they could not consider returning to Afghanistan until their daughters could be sure of receiving an education and unless women were allowed to work. Female employment has proved to be a necessity for many families in the camps and the prospect of having to survive in Afghanistan without this option, given the harsh economic conditions, has been a clear disincentive to return. However, the increased pressure on refugees in Pakistan that preceded the events of September 11 was reducing the element of choice in this matter.

The ban on female education has been linked to the drawing up of an appropriate education curriculum, in order to ensure that the next generation is brought up on the basis of an acceptable system of belief. The creation of a new curriculum is said to be conditional on the Taliban first taking full control of Afghanistan and then calling on a body of Ulema to determine its content. The present curriculum, which was drafted by the Mujahidin parties and therefore could be seen as already consistent with Islam, is not regarded as acceptable.

In answer to their critics, the Taliban state that they accept the mandatory nature of both female and male education but insist that the conditions must be right for that education to take place. There were, nevertheless, statements by senior people within the Taliban that girls' schools in Kabul might open by the spring of 1997, building on the small initiatives in areas such as Paktia, Ghazni and Kandahar, where girls' schools are already operating. However, the spring of 1997 came and went and only boys' schools were allowed to function.

The Taliban are not unusual within the Islamic world in insisting on conformity to a particular code of dress. However, they are at the extreme end in the degree to which they enforce this. The periodic practice by some elements within the Taliban, particularly the religious police, of beating women with sticks in the street if they do not comply has had an enormous impact on the mobility of the female population. There has, very evidently, been a climate of fear and this has inhibited women from leaving their homes unless it has been absolutely necessary. Thus even health workers, although permitted to work, have either abandoned their jobs or lived in hospitals for the full working week in order to minimise their exposure to the Taliban forces. There has also been a marked decline in women and children attending health facilities and this has been aggravated by moves to require women to attend only one hospital in Kabul designated for their use.

Having said that, there are differences between the cities, primarily Kabul and Herat, and other Taliban-controlled areas, with the Taliban forces in Kabul and Herat being generally more severe than those in other areas. There were reports of women being beaten while out shopping in Herat, which only stopped when the head of the religious police was temporarily transferred to other duties in April 1997. There was also a reported incident in January 1997 of a Western female aid worker being beaten in Herat for non-compliance with the requirement to wear a *burqa*. The Taliban apologised over this incident.

In fact, it has been far from clear to what extent such treatment of women by the religious police has been endorsed by the wider Taliban leadership. A number of statements issued from Kandahar have been highly critical of such behaviour. However, incidents of this kind have continued to happen, albeit without any obvious pattern. It has therefore been difficult to say, at any one time, whether the situation was deteriorating or whether the police were taking a more hands-off attitude.

One problem has been that the footsoldiers have taken a simplistic view of the Taliban gender policy; it has thus been easier to implement an absolute prohibition on women working than to grapple with nuances as to whether it is appropriate for women to work in particular sectors or with foreign agencies. For the vast majority of the footsoldiers, Kabul, for all its relative conservatism, is seen as decadent and corrupt. By extension, foreign agencies or women who work are seen as beyond the pale.

The Taliban have also been relatively extreme in requiring that women's faces be covered. The Mujahidin parties have never insisted that women wear the *burqa*, although its use has been widespread in the areas under Mujahidin control. In other parts of the Islamic world women are, at the most, required to cover part of the face, either by wearing masks over the eyes, or by leaving only their eyes exposed. Even within Afghanistan, the *burqa* is an urban phenomenon. Women in the villages wear headscarves except when they go into town, when a *burqa* is donned if they possess one. The imposition of the *burqa* has placed an additional financial burden on urban families at a time when the economy has been deteriorating. Very many families have been unable to afford *burqas* and women have tended to borrow the garment from others if they have had to go out, further inhibiting movement.

The movement of men outside the home has also been constrained by the imposition of the strict dress code. Men have needed to buy new clothes, and cloth for turbans, again during a period of economic hardship. Not all men have had the capacity to sport a full growth of beard. Men have not wanted to lay themselves open to the possibility of being picked up by the Taliban on the grounds of non-conformity with the dress code in case they are then arrested on suspicion of being linked with the opposition forces or accused of corruption.

The gender policies of the Taliban need to be looked at in the context of the development of gender-related policies since the beginning of the twentieth century, the use of gender as a key focus of the Mujahidin parties, and the different forms that gender policies have taken within radical Islam.

Within traditional society, women have largely been accorded the roles of wives and mothers, to which has been added an important economic role covering certain aspects of the agricultural routine, particularly planting and weeding, animal husbandry and craft production. Men have covered other parts of the agricultural process and have also played a role in child care. They have also tended to take responsibility for the shopping. However, women have been seen as the primary vehicle for passing Islam from one generation to the next.

Women have, in addition, had an important symbolic role as the core or heart of society. This has been particularly the case in the legal code of the Pushtuns, Pushtunwali, where the protection of women is bound up with the protection of society. Similarly, the honour of society is dependent on the honour of women. For example, in Pushtun tribal society, if a woman has been disgraced by being assaulted by a member of another tribe, the tribe to which she belongs has the right to exact vengeance.

Within Pushtun society the wish to protect women has traditionally resulted in their movement being circumscribed, to a greater or lesser extent, so that they have at best limited contact with men outside the family or village community and, if they have such contact, it must be on the basis of clearly defined rules. This restriction on the contact which women have had with the outside world has been given the name of purdah.

In the centre and north of Afghanistan, other traditions have dictated the mobility of women, with strong influences from Central Asia, from which significant elements of the population have migrated. Turkoman women are very constrained in their movements. The movement of women in the Hazara, Uzbek and Tajik societies has also been circumscribed, but not to the degree inherent in Pushtun society. Nomadic women are an important exception to the norm. In nomadic society, women are inevitably highly mobile and do not face the strict taboos on contact with strangers that exist in Pushtunwali and some other subcultures.

In Afghanistan as a whole, both women and men have traditionally conformed to certain codes of dress regarded as appropriate in order to ensure modesty. Women have normally worn a *shalwar kameez* and, in addition, either worn a *burqa*, otherwise known as a *chadri*, a garment that covers the whole body, including the face, or a loose cloth that envelops the body and covers the hair. In traditional rural society, the *burqa* was seldom worn because it interfered with women's work in the fields and with the care of livestock. The garment originated in the urban areas and was designed to put all women in public on an equal basis and to keep women from being coveted by other men. However, as some villages grew into towns and developed bazaars, women from the outlying villages felt it to be a sign of sophistication to wear a *burqa*. Its use thus increased in the rural areas while urban women gravitated towards more Western styles. The *burqa* has been more common in the southern provinces but has none the less been in widespread use in the north.

Men have traditionally been expected to wear *shalwar kameez* and some form of head covering, depending on the region. In some areas, it has been expected that men would be bearded. In certain parts of Afghanistan it has been the custom to grow the hair long, while in others short hair has been the norm. Western clothing has been worn by a minority of the population and for a relatively short period, historically.

King Amanullah's reforms offended conservative opinion by including a number of measures designed to improve the position of women and girls and to change gender-related customs. He banned child marriage, transferred the regulation of family affairs from the clergy to the state, outlawed polygamy among civil servants, permitted women to discard the veil and required men living in or visiting Kabul to wear Western dress, including a European hat. In 1928 a hundred women, led by the queen, appeared at a public function unveiled. Amanullah's rulings were annulled once Habibullah II took power and the Ulema later, under Habibullah II's successor, issued a ruling that, based on their interpretation of Shari'a law, women were not allowed to vote – a right they did not, in any event, enjoy.

It was not until Daoud Khan became prime minister in 1953 that any further initiatives were taken to improve the position of women. In 1957 female singers and presenters were heard on Kabul Radio. The following year, the government sent a female delegate to the United Nations in New York. At the same time, women were employed as hostesses and receptionists at the national airline and were unveiled. In 1959, Daoud repeated Amanullah's earlier initiative by having the wives and daughters of senior government officials appear unveiled on a review stand at the independence day celebrations. When the Ulema objected, he challenged them to find indisputable evidence in the Shari'a to justify the veil. They were not able to do this but campaigned vociferously against him, expressing their fear that the growing presence of Soviet advisers would undermine Islam. However Daoud, with the army behind him, was able to stand his ground.

He was helped by the global intellectual movements of the 1960s, which challenged existing thinking and resulted in pressure from some quarters for women to be accorded greater rights and freedoms. A growing number of girls benefited from secondary and higher education and this in turn provoked a reaction from the Ulema, who argued that the expansion of non-traditional education was eroding the morals of the young and undermining traditional social values. They drew ideological justification from the work of the Pakistani Islamic theorist Abdul Ala Maududi, who insisted that women should be fully veiled when leaving the home, and that men and women should be segregated. The presence of Western hippies in Afghanistan during that period enhanced their anxieties over what they saw as declining moral standards.

The government set up by the People's Democratic Republic of Afghanistan, through the coup of April 1978, took the reform process a substantial step further by seeking to impose female education throughout the country in an effort to combat the very high level of illiteracy. However, its initiatives met with fierce opposition from traditional leaders in the rural areas, and this was a major factor in the emergence of the resistance to the PDPA regime that provoked the Soviet invasion. There was particular concern that girls would be taught on the basis of an alien value system rather than, as had been the practice, through the religious instruction given by older women in the villages. The removal of village mullahs from the education system also aroused considerable alarm amongst religious and traditional leaders. This resistance was built upon by the seven Mujahidin parties, particularly the Islamist parties. These parties placed the protection of women at the forefront of their objectives and drew on the thinking of radical Islamists such as Maududi to strengthen their own ideological position.

For many of the six million refugees who fled to Pakistan or Iran as a result of the PDPA coup and the subsequent Soviet invasion, fear that their daughters would be influenced by a secular ideology was a major factor, consistent with the declaration of the jihad, in their decision to leave Afghanistan. (Many years later, urban dwellers left Afghanistan following the collapse of the Najibullah government in April 1992 and the emergence of the Mujahidin government, out of concern that their daughters would have to conform to a stricter interpretation of Islam.)

The resistance to the Soviet invasion was, therefore, presented as a resistance to both Western and socialist influences. The socialist system was seen as potentially undermining Islam because of its secular nature. Western society was viewed in a similar light, in part because of the distinction drawn between the state and religion, with religion being relegated to the private sphere, and in part because Western society had been presented to the public as decadent. On both counts it was feared that women would, at best, abandon their Muslim values and, at worst, slide into immoral behaviour.

This attitude created an ambivalance within the population towards Western humanitarian aid agencies. (An interesting parallel can be seen with the early history of Islam where, having taken new areas, the Muslim conquerors found themselves dependent on Christians to run the administration, fuelling internal debate as to whether these Christians would undermine the values the movements were seeking to impart.) There was a fear that if the agencies had contact with Afghan women, either as recipients of aid or as employees, these women would be corrupted. Western women working for the agencies had to be careful to dress appropriately and would normally wear *shalwar kameez* and a headscarf. Agencies tended to use their non-Afghan female staff to work with Afghan female staff or recipients in order to minimise problems.

To some extent the Mujahidin parties used the presence of the foreign agencies to strengthen their own positions. By presenting the agencies as a potential threat to Islam and to Afghan society, through the corrupting influence they might have on Afghan women, they gave the agencies a symbolic importance in the public eye. Thus, when a particular mullah gave a sermon in one of the refugee camps and reported a rumour that a certain foreign agency had converted an Afghan woman to Christianity, he provoked a mob attack on all the buildings held by the agency in the camp and these were burned to the ground.

During the early years after the departure of the Soviet forces, humanitarian agencies found themselves under frequent verbal attacks from some of the Mujahidin parties and from Islamist fringe movements, and it was common for Afghan women working for the agencies to receive threats. Some left their work as a result of these threats. Others continued, either out of defiance or because they needed to work in order to maintain their families.

The debates that have taken place in Afghanistan have their echoes in Iran. There, when Ayatollah Khomeini took power, there was much discussion as to whether women should be obliged to wear the traditional *burqa* or be permitted to wear long loose clothing and headscarves. The *burqa* was not adopted. The priority to be given to female education also aroused controversy, although, in the end, a high level of provision was made. Arguments as to whether women should be allowed to work resulted in a compromise that they could work provided that they had the permission of their husbands.

It is also of interest to note the position of the Muslim Brotherhood ideologue, Muhammad Ghazali, in view of the significant influence of the Brotherhood on the Islamist movement in Afghanistan prior to the Soviet invasion. Writing in 1948 in *Our Beginning in Wisdom*, he proposed a ban on what could be regarded as seductive clothing or appearance in women and on their presence unchaperoned at picnics and outings. He was in favour of female education provided it was geared exclusively to their designated role of bringing up children.

Elsewhere in the Islamic world, there has been a wide range of interpretations of the Qur'an and the Hadith as to how women should dress and generally involve themselves in society. There are strong contrasts between, for example, Saudi Arabia, where women are heavily veiled and are not permitted to drive cars, and other parts of the Middle East, where women are able to play a reasonably full role in the public sphere, comparable with the West. There are similar contrasts within countries between urban and rural communities and between those espousing radical Islamic ideologies and those taking a more moderate or liberal position. There has been, throughout the Islamic world, a growing trend for Muslim women to wear a form of head covering, resembling a nun's habit, and long coats, in order to assert their allegiance to Islam. In Algeria, Islamic radicals have targeted women who have not conformed to such a dress code.

There has equally been a range of responses amongst Afghan women to women's role within Afghan society and within Islam, covering the full spectrum from radical Islam to a secular position. For example, the Revolutionary Afghan Women's Association takes the middle ground in advocating that women should play a full role in the political life of the country and have the same access as men to education, training and employment, while remaining within the Islamic fold. The organisation thus expects women to conform to an appropriately decorous form of dress but does not insist on the *burqa*.

The debate as to how women should behave and participate in society has been going on for a very long time and it has perhaps been the cause of more controversy than any other issue since the beginning of the twentieth century. When the Taliban took power in Kandahar in October 1994, they were therefore opting for a position in a pre-existing discussion.

Being predominantly Pushtun and rural in their composition, they were inevitably influenced by the code of honour prescribed in Pushtun law, which determined that women should live in purdah and be protected from the outside world. The Taliban governor of Herat expressed their position very clearly, in an interview given on 8 October to a correspondent of Voice of the Islamic Republic of Iran, External Service, Tehran, broadcast in Pashto:

> It is a matter of pride for all Afghanistan that we have kept our women at home ... The Shari'a has described everyone's way of conduct. I mean that the Shari'a allows for a woman to see a male doctor when she becomes ill. The fact of the matter is that no other country has given women the rights we have given them. We have given women the rights that God and his Messenger have instructed, that is to stay in their homes and to gain religious instruction in *hejab* [seclusion].

The Taliban were also much influenced by the positions taken within the Harakat party of the Mujahidin and by those adopted by the Ulema and the mullahs who fought the rearguard action against the Amanullah government during the early part of the twentieth century. In many respects, they have therefore been seeking a return to the situation that existed before the 1960s. Thus, in prohibiting women from working, the Taliban consider that they are freeing society of what they see as the corrupt influences that have crept in as a consequence of Daoud's reforms, the PDPA coup and the fourteen years of Soviet-backed governments, the period of rule by the Islamist parties and the presence of Western agencies.

Their awareness of developments within Afghanistan during the twentieth century is also likely to have coloured the Taliban attitude to female education. Education has been explicitly used as a tool to impart particular ideologies, starting with King Amanullah's attempts to modernise Afghanistan through the education system. Daoud, the PDPA and the Islamist parties of the Mujahidin followed his example. Saudi Arabia (through the funding of educational institutions), the Islamist parties in Pakistan and a number of smaller political movements in the region have all seized the opportunity created by the conflict to promote their ideologies through educational institutions and orphanages.

There is concern that girls will be corrupted by anything other than a pure Islamic teaching, consistent with the Taliban interpretation of Islam, and a consequent wish to create an exclusive focus on what is seen as their important role of bringing up the next generation of pure Muslims.

Some of the elements within the Islamic world that are opposed to the Taliban for political or strategic reasons have taken the opportunity created by international reactions to Taliban gender policies to level public criticism at them. On 2 October a representative of Pakistan's Jamaat-i-Islami party, which has played a major role in supporting the Islamist parties within the Mujahidin, issued a statement in which he said that the Taliban decrees barring women from education and employment, ordering women to wear the veil and requiring men to grow beards could give a negative image of Islam. He said there was no justification within Islamic law for many of the measures announced by the Taliban, and added that the Muslim faith made the education of females mandatory and that women should also be allowed to work, so long as they observed Islamic norms of dress and behaviour. The position taken by Jamaat-i-Islami is of interest, given the key role played by Maududi in its formation. Other smaller religious movements in Pakistan have expressed similar views and have pointed out that girls and boys can be educated in separate schools but must have equal resources.

The policies of the Taliban have created particular dilemmas for Western agencies and the international community, who have inevitably responded to them from a Western perspective as well as on the basis of the UN Human Rights Conventions. Because Western society is relatively individualistic, each individual, female or male, will normally seek fulfilment on the basis of personal life choices. For most, these life choices relate to employment options. Life choices also include deciding whether or not to have children and, if so, how many. Social pressures still influence these choices in the West such that women are expected to have children but, increasingly, women are putting off having their first child until they are in their thirties and will normally limit the number of children they have. The pressure to have or not have children is not geared to a perpetuation of the culture or religion, with the possible exception of Roman Catholics, or to the advancement of the nation, although it does relate to societal status. Such an approach to life has existed in Afghanistan, but only amongst a small minority over a relatively short period, and many of these have long since left the country for the West. However, Western observers spontaneously identify with this minority.

It is also important to recognise that Western society is no more homogeneous than Afghan society. There are differences between women in Afghanistan based on ethnicity, religion, access to income and urban or rural settlement, just as within the West there are significant differences based on nationality, class, age, income and environment. The personality of the individual also plays a key part in both Afghan and Western societies. Any dialogue has, therefore, to be based on a respect for the values that participants in the dialogue adhere to. It is not appropriate for Westerners to deny their own values any more than it is acceptable for them to be dismissive of societal values in Afghanistan. The difficulty arises when one or both parties to a dialogue is taking what is regarded as an extreme or rigid position. One then has to ask why such a position is being taken, what the possible historical causes of such a position are, and whether there are factors in addition to the simple question of values.

It may be useful, in this context, to reflect on the concept of otherness, whereby groups form to differentiate themselves from other groups. The recent history of Afghanistan has seen this process in an acute form but there have been similar episodes in European and American history. Present Western societies are also characterised by group relationships based on differential access to power as well as on different interests and identities. When groups feel threatened, attutudes within them tend to harden and they seek to define more clearly the aspects of their identity that differentiate them from other groups. Where nationalist or religious identity has been involved, women have often taken on a symbolic importance as the reproducers of that identity . This has been a particular characteristic of Muslim societies under threat, such as that in Algeria, and amongst Muslim communities in European cities. However, there is also the more pervasive threat created by mass communication, which introduces a certain image of Western culture into homes throughout the world and is often felt to be insidiously undermining of other cultures.

Afghanistan is one of the few places left in the world where Western media do not penetrate to a significant degree. The rigidity of the Taliban gender policies could be seen as a desperate attempt to keep out that other world, and to protect Afghan women from influences that could weaken the society from within.

9 The Dialogue with the Humanitarian Agencies

The benefits of the economic assistance provided by the Soviet Union, the USA and Europe during the post-war years were quickly lost as the Soviet forces reduced highways to pot-holed obstacle courses and devastated agriculture through sustained bombing campaigns. As the Soviet troops withdrew in February 1989, those displaced within Afghanistan began to return to their villages to embark on the long process of reconstruction. For many, mine clearance was the first task and, lacking specialist assistance, they did the best they could, with inevitable casualties. The rebuilding of houses was also a priority. People helped each other with this, as they did with the clearing of irrigation canals and the preparation of land for cultivation.

However, there came a point where technical expertise from outside was needed. Improved seed varieties were required. Engineers were needed to design flood protection structures and irrigation systems that would enable communities to make the leap from a marginal level of survival to economic self-sufficiency.

UN agencies and non-governmental organisations (NGOs) were ready to assist from the date of the Soviet pull-out. NGOs already had long experience of providing aid to enable impoverished populations in the rural areas of Afghanistan to survive. The Soviet invasion of December 1979 had brought back memories of the 1956 invasion of Hungary and met with strong reactions from the international community. It also aroused empathy among those who had experienced Nazi occupation during the Second World War. Solidarity committees sprung up on the European mainland, in the UK and in North America. The Soviet occupation of Afghanistan created equally strong reactions in the Islamic world, alarmed by an assault on fellow Muslims by a secular force. Collections were organised in mosques in support of the Mujahidin.

Many of the solidarity committees organised themselves to deliver relief supplies to Afghanistan, and they were joined by established aid organisations from both the Islamic world and the West.

The humanitarian assistance organisations worked largely through Mujahidin commanders, providing cash and wheat to them for distribution to communities within Afghanistan. From 1986 onwards, the funding available increased significantly as USAID arrived on the scene and offered grants to NGOs for humanitarian assistance programmes. This coincided with a dramatic increase in US military support to the Mujahidin. Sympathisers from both the West and the Islamic world found themselves supporting a resistance movement in which radical Islam was the binding force. They therefore had to accommodate themselves to an ideology with which they were not necessarily in agreement and one that envisaged a more defined and restricted role for women than was the norm in most of the world.

As the Soviet withdrawal proceeded the agencies set in motion plans to support a mass repatriation of the six million refugees from Pakistan and Iran, believing that the Najibullah government would fall in the immediate wake of Soviet withdrawal. When this did not happen, the agencies moved into a more gradual process of preparing for an eventual return by rehabilitating the principal areas from which the refugees originated.

Much of the assistance was geared to a restoration of the agricultural base. Priority was given to the repair of irrigation and flood protection structures and to the provision of improved wheat seed and tree saplings. Large programmes were also set up to provide health and veterinary care. At the same time a major operation was established to survey and clear mines from roads, canals and agricultural land. In the urban areas, agencies worked on water supply, sanitation, health and relief programmes.

To provide aid to the rural districts, agencies had to negotiate with Mujahidin commanders and militia leaders. Over time, they extended the discussion process to include the wider community. Village structures thus became the preferred operating partners, with the beneficiaries of aid taking responsibility for the provision of resources along with the agencies. Similarly, in the cities, agencies worked in partnership with the remnants of government ministries and municipalities in order to ensure that agency interventions were consistent with the plans and priorities of the local administration. Where possible they also worked with neighbourhood structures, on the same basis as with village structures. The discussions with administrative, village or neighbourhood structures on the planning and implementation of programmes would often continue for a considerable period. There was, therefore, an inevitable regard for cultural and religious factors in the consideration of programmes.

This dialogue with governmental and community-based structures, as well as with the Mujahidin commanders, also involved an acceptance of Western and other Islamic value systems. Agencies came with their own mandates, principles and objectives and these determined the nature of the assistance they were willing to provide and the conditions under which they would give aid. Similarly, the beneficiaries were already engaged in a process of rehabilitation based on their own objectives and value systems and, while they welcomed the assistance provided, they were not prepared to accept this at any price.

The issue of how to consult with women and how to ensure that they benefited equally from the assistance provided was a difficult one from the very beginning. It was less difficult in negotiations with community-based structures in villages, where the cultural norms were well established and where there was therefore more flexibility, than in discussions with representatives of the Mujahidin parties. With the latter, because the question of women's seclusion was an element in their political ideology, there was at times a pronounced rigidity in response to requests from agencies that women should be consulted, involved and derive equal benefit.

Western NGOs have therefore been very cautious about how they have worked with women, both as recipients of aid and as staff. They have made every effort to conform with cultural norms but they have also sought to ensure that women benefited equally, as far as possible, from the aid given and that they were consulted as to the nature of the aid. They would, for example, discuss with the male representatives of traditional structures in the villages and in the refugee camps how access to women could appropriately be achieved and how women might be involved in the decision-making process. Female staff, both Afghan and expatriate, were also engaged to facilitate access to women.

However, it has proved extremely difficult to ensure that women have had equal access to aid. The task has been easier in some areas of assistance. For example one could reasonably argue that women might benefit as much as men from work to restore the agricultural base. It was also possible to target women through vaccination programmes or mother and child health clinics. However, it was often difficult to ensure that women benefited equally from relief programmes or from medical services provided through clinics serving the whole population. The provision of education for girls was inevitably much less than that for boys because of cultural norms and the sensitivities prevailing.

Western NGOs have also been very cautious about how they have involved themselves in the education field because of the sensitivity of the Mujahidin parties to any Western involvement in education. The attempts by the PDPA government to impose a socialist system of education left deep scars in the rural population, and neither the Mujahidin parties nor the village or refugee camp structures have been prepared to take any risks with Western agencies. However, the Islamic NGOs have not been so constrained and have operated primary and secondary schools, universities and orphanages, with freedom to determine the curriculum.

The Western NGOs operated in accordance with a curriculum drawn up jointly by a USAID-funded project run by the University of Omaha at Nebraska and the Pakistan-based Afghan Interim Government of the Mujahidin parties. Common textbooks were published and were distributed to schools throughout Afghanistan. NGOs assisted with the repair and construction of school buildings and provided financial support for the payment of teachers' salaries and to cover the costs of materials. When the Taliban took over Kandahar, agencies were therefore already adapting to gender and other policies that were not significantly more liberal than those of the Taliban. They were also used to negotiating on the basis of these policies, and so were hopeful that it would be possible to negotiate with the Taliban as they had done with the Mujahidin parties.

The experience of NGOs working in Kandahar during the early period after the Taliban takeover confirmed that dialogue was possible. Agencies working in the health sector expressed concern to the Taliban that they were not able to provide health care to women because of the ban on female employment. Discussions took place over a period and resulted in agreement that women could be employed in health programmes. The discussions covered the cultural restrictions on women having contact with men outside the family, and the consequent difficulties inherent in the use of male medical staff. When the Taliban took over other areas of Afghanistan, the authority for women to work in the health sector was automatically extended to these areas.

It was also possible for expatriate female NGO staff to work on a day-to-day basis with the Ministry of Health in Kandahar, although there was some initial resistance. NGOs made it clear that it was their policy to work with the government ministries in order to comply with the policies and plans prevailing and to engage in the joint planning of services. However, when the Taliban took Herat, female expatriate NGO staff found that there was a block on their meeting their counterparts in the government ministries. Agencies were also unable to negotiate any further concessions with the Taliban, particularly in relation to the employment of women in non-health posts and to the provision of female education, in spite of the dramatic impact the ban on female employment and education had in Herat. This difference between Kandahar and Herat in the willingness of the Taliban to be flexible in their discussions with the agencies appeared to result from a more conservative leadership in Herat, and from the greater difficulties the Taliban faced in seeking to consolidate their hold on Herat as compared with Kandahar.

Agencies working in the education field in Herat had their programmes seriously curtailed. UNICEF, for example, had been distributing educational materials to schools. Suddenly a large proportion of the schools were no longer operating, either because they were exclusively for girls or because they could not function after the loss of their female staff. UNICEF debated the issue within its own structure and, with regret, came to the conclusion that it could not operate in accordance with its mandate. It opted to suspend its education programmes in all parts of Afghanistan where girls were denied access to education. Save the Children Fund (UK), which was repairing and building schools in Herat Province, found that it could not meet the requirements of its mandate if it could not employ women to consult and communicate with women, as the main carers of children. It felt it had no choice but to suspend its Herat programme.

Although only two agencies took the step of suspending their programmes, there was considerable reflection within other agencies and in meetings between agencies as to how best to respond to the restrictions on female education and employment. Agencies felt the issues should, theoretically, be negotiable because they were presented in the context of a belief system that was clearly stated as being based on Islam. They were aware that the Qur'an did not specifically prohibit female employment and that female education was mandatory. They were also aware that, although only a proportion of girls had benefited from education and a very much smaller proportion of women had worked, there was an acceptance within society at large that female education and employment were, to a degree, both desirable and necessary. However, they did not feel able to challenge the Taliban on the basis of their particular interpretation of the Qur'an, which was not fundamentally different from the one that had prevailed in Afghanistan during the early part of the century.

They also recognised that the Taliban were giving their full attention to the process of conquest and to the disarming of the population. Thus, while they were happy for the agencies to continue what they were doing, they would not be particularly bothered if the agencies chose to leave. There was therefore little or nothing to be gained by insisting that the Taliban modify their gender policy as a condition for the agencies deciding to remain.

The agencies opted to focus on operational concerns and to rely on the concept of charity inherent in Islam as a basis for negotiation. A consensus emerged between the agencies that dialogue should be maintained and that agencies should engage in discussion with the Taliban as to how the needs of vulnerable elements in the community could be met by the authorities and the agencies working together. It was agreed that a confrontational approach could be counter-productive and could present the debate as being between a Western liberal ideology and a radical Islamic one rather than one based on the practical and immediate needs of the population and the cultural and religious norms prevailing in Afghanistan.

The agencies, however, found some difficulty in reconciling the apparent indifference of the Taliban as to whether or not they stayed with the fact that they were effectively running many of the government services, since, when the Taliban arrived in Herat, the administration had lost a significant proportion of the few staff who remained. However, the agencies were ever mindful of the serious humanitarian needs, particularly of the urban population, and felt it their responsibility to remain.

When Kabul was taken, the agencies saw the opportunity to reopen negotiations on female access to education and employment and hoped that the relatively liberal elements within the Taliban would have more influence when faced with the complexities of running a government. They therefore moved quickly to negotiate with the Taliban as soon as Kabul was taken. There was, in any event, an urgency to the situation. The population of Kabul had suffered from a year of rapid inflation and food and fuel shortages as a result of the blockades imposed by Hekmatyar and the Taliban. Many were already near destitution, having sold basic possessions. An estimated 25,000 widows were dependent on regular relief supplies and several hundred thousand people were in receipt of subsidised bread from the World Food Programme and of substantial assistance from the International Committee of the Red Cross. The agencies also needed to continue employing their female staff in order to maintain their access to female beneficiaries, and the ban on female employment had seriously curtailed agency operations.

The UN agencies and NGOs operating in Kabul met on 5 October 1996 to draw up a position statement. This included the following values and beliefs:

- International agencies believe in humanitarian principles. These principles underpin all our plans and programmes that are designed to relieve the poverty, distress and suffering of the people of Afghanistan.
- International agencies are neutral in their provision of services. We do not favour any group on the basis of political or religious affiliation. As such we are non-partisan.
- International agencies believe in maintaining and promoting the inherent equality and dignity of all people, and do not discrimimate between the sexes, races, ethnic groups or religions.

- International agencies hold local customs and cultures in high respect.

After expanding further on its operational modalities, which included the involvement of all members of communities in the design, implementation and monitoring of projects and the wish of agencies to coordinate with the responsible authorities, the statement requested the authorities in Kabul to act with all possible urgency on the following issues:

- All female agency staff must be allowed to return to work in their respective agencies in order to achieve each agency's goals and undertake its planned and ongoing activities.
- In programmes where women and children are affected, they must be allowed to have unrestricted access to, and participate in, all programme plans and activities.
- International agencies request the Afghan authorities to provide equal access to education and training opportunities for females and males at all levels in order to ensure the long-term development of Afghanistan.
- We request the authorities to ensure the personal safety of all agency staff so that agencies can achieve their humanitarian goals and objectives.
- International agencies reserve the sole right to select and employ staff at all levels according to their suitability for the job.
- International agencies request equal access to the authorities for all agency representatives, irrespective of gender, so that they can liaise with the authorities on an equal footing.
- We request that early consideration be given to establish the way for basic agreements between international agencies and government, so that longer-term humanitarian assistance can be provided to the people of Afghanistan on a mutually agreed, legal basis.

A meeting was held between representatives of the agencies and the Taliban acting foreign minister, Haji Mawlawi Muhammad Ghaus Akhund, on 8 September, less than two weeks after the Taliban takeover of Kabul. The delegation, which included two women, expressed the concern of the agencies that nearly all their projects in the city had had to be suspended because of the restrictions on the employment of women, and that agencies had no access to the most vulnerable people in the city. The agencies stated their fear that a tragedy would result.

The minister responded that the priority of the Taliban was to bring peace and security to the whole country and to establish a strong, central Islamic government. He indicated that when the Taliban regime was accorded international recognition, responses to other issues would be clarified. He said that two sets of values impinged upon the Taliban at the present time, international and national, and expressed the hope that the UN and international agencies would not insist too much on traditions that were contrary to national values. He observed that only 2 per cent of women nationwide worked in offices and asked why they should focus on this 2 per cent. The agencies responded that they needed to employ this 2 per cent in order to gain access to the significant number of women who were vulnerable. The minister agreed to consider the issues raised and to come back to the agencies.

The situation since the meeting has been extremely confused. Some agencies have been given authority, either verbally or in writing, to employ women for certain types of programmes. However, an edict issued at one point contradicted this and placed a total ban on the employment of Afghan women by foreign agencies. Agencies then reopened negotiations and some were able to achieve a degree of flexibility. Particular problems have arisen because the Department for the Promotion of Virtue and the Prevention of Vice and the Ministry of Justice have clearly taken a much harder line than other elements of the Taliban in terms of how much flexibility should be permitted. Agencies operating in other parts of the country have encountered a mixed picture, with very different approaches and attitudes being manifested by Taliban representatives regarding both female employment and education. As these representatives have changed, so the local policies have changed.

What, then, are the choices open to agencies in a situation such as this? At one extreme, they can choose to disregard the political and human rights situation, on the grounds that the level of humanitarian need is so great they have a duty to do what they can, overcoming whatever obstacles present themselves. They may consider, however, either that their mandate prevents them taking such a position, or that the situation is seriously affecting the economic survival of the population to the point where they must speak out. Both situations have arisen in Afghanistan. UNICEF has felt unable to continue with its education programmes because of inconsistencies within its mandates. The UN and other agencies have responded to clear evidence in Kabul that the restrictions imposed by the Taliban have affected the ability of households to survive economically, and have expressed their concern to the authorities.

If agencies decide that they cannot disregard human rights abuses, they have a number of choices. They can close their programmes completely. They can suspend them, as the Save the Children Fund (UK) did in Herat, or put them on hold, the option chosen by the UN High Commissioner for Refugees when some of its staff were arrested, pending an improvement in the human rights situation. Alternatively they can continue to operate, while expressing their concern to the authorities and drawing their attention to the implications of the human rights abuses for the population and for the agency's programme. However, the latter option can carry certain risks. It may weaken the collective stand of agencies, aimed at putting pressure on the authorities to improve the human rights situation. In some contexts, the agency may also put the safety of its staff at risk. On the other hand, by negotiating on the basis of actual operations agencies can, in some circumstances, exert greater leverage on the authorities to improve their human rights record than they could if they suspended their programmes. Agencies suspending their programmes may find that the authorities are preoccupied with military matters and do not care whether the agency remains or not, so cannot be bothered with discussions over principles. However, discussions based on pragmatic concerns may be felt to be a sufficient priority.

One of the difficulties agencies have faced in seeking to maintain a common position is that the Taliban have behaved more punitively in Kabul than in other areas controlled by them. For example, agencies operating in Jalalabad initially found a greater willingness to compromise on the question of female employment than those in Kabul. In discussions between agencies operating in different parts of Afghanistan, the differing perceptions agencies bring to the debate make it harder to arrive at a common position.

Another major difficulty in maintaining a common stance is that the situation is fluid. The Taliban have, at various times, given statements

or permitted changes in agency practice that indicated a possible soften-
ing in their policy on gender. However, these have been sometimes
contradicted or ignored by others in the movement, signalling a possible
reversal in the process of change. Agencies have been at a loss as to
whether to conclude that there is a positive process of change over
time, albeit with some reversals, or whether nothing is really changing.
The increasingly tense situation that has developed since the Taliban
failed to take Mazar in May 1997 has further complicated agency assessments of whether there is a gradual improvement in gender policy.

Agencies have legitimacy to express their views only in so far as they
are actors within the local environment. It is thus difficult for them to
argue that women should have the right to personal fulfilment in their
lives through access to employment. However, they can reasonably
contend that they need to employ women with a certain educational
level and with particular technical skills to meet stated needs for which
they, the agencies, have taken on responsibility. They can equally argue
that, in their efforts to tackle poverty or health problems, limitations on
female access to employment or health care are detrimental to the
welfare of women and children.

International donors have had to grapple with the same problems
and to decide under what conditions they have been willing to provide
funding. Increasingly, donors have been meeting the agencies to discuss
possible options.

These dilemmas are faced in other conflict areas, where agencies and
donors have necessarily had to make compromises with their mandates
and principles in the face of what are termed complex emergencies.
Lessons learned from these situations indicate that agencies should give
priority to informing themselves as much as possible on the complexities
around them, and to coordinating well with other agencies in the
planning of programmes. However, it is in dealing with the unknown
elements that the greatest problems arise. Up to the present time, the
Taliban movement has been too diffuse for agencies to make reasonable
assessments about appropriate strategies to adopt in modifying their
policies. In short, there are often too many variables for agencies to be
able to make informed decisions.

The spring and summer of 1997 saw a number of measures by the
Taliban to restrict female employment and access to health services. It

became necessary to lay off a large number of Afghan women working for NGO health programmes, and many health clinics had to be closed. Tensions were increased when the European Union's commissioner for humanitarian affairs, Emma Bonino, visited Kabul in September 1997. She was arrested and held for three hours after the religious police objected to accompanying journalists filming in a womens' hospital. In an increasingly tense environment, the Taliban then, in July 1998, issued an order requiring all NGOs to relocate to a derelict polytechnic building in an area of Kabul that was felt by the agencies to be insecure. Agencies expressed their opposition to the proposal and sought to negotiate. When negotiations broke down and the deadline for the expulsion by the Taliban of the NGOs from Kabul was approaching, Emma Bonino sent a letter to all the NGOs funded by ECHO in Kabul informing them that they would no longer receive funding if they remained.

The departure of NGOs from Kabul in July 1998 dramatically reduced the capacity of the humanitarian community to respond to the considerable needs in the capital. Although agencies gradually trickled back over the following year, programmes in the capital have never returned to the scale that had existed prior to July 1998.

However, in the rural areas, programming continued much as before and it proved possible to further consolidate initiatives to undertake more long-term work in support of the efforts of village communities to strengthen the agricultural infrastructure. Thus, when a serious drought hit the country in 2000, the effects were mitigated in many areas by the groundwork already undertaken. However, agencies were not in a position to reach all the affected villages and hundreds of thousands of people opted to move to the urban centres in the hope of benefiting from the food aid that was made available.

The UN sanctions imposed in December 2000, which were far more far-reaching than those of October 1999, had the effect of significantly radicalising the political environment, thus giving greater influence over policy to hardliners within the movement. One of the effects of this was that there was much greater antipathy towards Western agencies, manifested in increasing controls over their operations, and some agencies that the Taliban felt particularly uneasy about were asked to leave in August 2001.

The terrorist attacks on US targets of September 11, 2001 led humanitarian agencies to withdraw their expatriate staff because of fears for their security but programmes were able to continue, albeit at a much reduced capacity, through the local staff of agencies already operating in the country.

10 The Taliban and the International Community

> ... 'culture' is never an essentialist and homogeneous body of traditions and customs, but a rich resource, usually full of internal contradictions, and a resource which is always used selectively in various ethnic, cultural and religious projects within specific power relations and political discourse (Nira Yuval-Davis, 1997: 38).

Mujahidin fighters travelling over the mountains of Afghanistan during the 1980s would often have been accompanied by a Western journalist on a donkey, dressed in the full paraphernalia of *shalwar kameez* and headcovering. Reporting on the heroic exploits of the glorious freedom fighters, the journalists were able to give a highly simplistic message of military prowess in the face of overwhelming odds.

The day the Soviet troops left Afghanistan, the tune changed. The image of the Mujahidin became one of reactionaries, fighting amongst themselves and unable to form a government. The situation was suddenly complex. It was difficult to understand who was fighting whom, and why. The media lost interest, and it seemed as though the rest of the world no longer had an interest in what happened in this remote corner.

The emergence of the Taliban in October 1994 attracted media attention because of their remarkable success in capturing a large area in a very short time, and because their explicit denial of female access to education and employment and the imposition of ultra-conservative dress codes made news. Over the next couple of years there was a constant low level of media coverage, including some documentaries in which the impact of the Taliban was assessed. The capture of Kabul and the immediate hanging of Najibullah and his brother presented powerful and dramatic images onto which the media latched. Much of the coverage was negative, but some journalists did report on the popularity of the Taliban in the southern provinces and on the initial relief of the population of Kabul that the days of rocketing and blockades might at last be over.

In the face of this intense media coverage, which highlighted the immediate bans placed on female education and employment and the difficulties humanitarian agencies were facing as a result, the UN felt it had to issue a statement. Together with the European Parliament, it brought the UN Human Rights Conventions into the debate, condemning the gender policies of the Taliban as human rights violations.

On 3 October 1996 the European Union's commissioner for humanitarian affairs, Emma Bonino, said in an interview that the rights of women must be respected in Afghanistan before there could be any international recognition of the new Taliban government in Kabul. The following day, the UN human rights commissioner, José Ayala-Lasso, said in a prepared statement that he had urged his representative in Kabul urgently to convey to the Taliban his 'strong concern for the situation of human rights in Afghanistan'. He appealed to the Taliban 'to ensure respect for such rights as the rights of women to work and the rights of girls to education', noting that Afghanistan had signed various conventions to protect women's rights.

On 8 October the UN secretary-general issued a statement in which he said that all UN assistance had to be guided by the UN Charter, which affirmed equal rights for men and women. The same day, the USA warned the Taliban administration that it would not secure international recognition or aid unless it respected the rights of women.

On 9 October the executive director of UNICEF, Carol Bellamy, announced that UNICEF was suspending its assistance to educational programmes in Kabul, adding that these programmes would only be reinstated when the Taliban accepted that girls had a right to attend school. This suspension was an extension of one issued in response to the ban imposed on female education when the Taliban took Herat in September 1995.

On 17 October the UN Security Council issued a resolution in which it expressed concern at what it described as extreme discrimination against women and urged strict adherence to the norms of international humanitarian law. It also called for an immediate ceasefire in Afghanistan and urged all Afghan parties to begin a dialogue in cooperation with the UN. It further appealed for an end to outside interference in Afghanistan and for states to prevent the flow of new arms into the country.

On 24 October the European Parliament adopted a resolution in which it called on all states to oppose the Taliban administration in Kabul because of what it called systematic discrimination against Afghan women, the numerous violations of human rights and the forcible indoctrination of the Afghan people. It noted that the repression against women conflicted with the 1979 International Convention on the Elimination of All Forms of Discrimination Against Women and the 1966 Treaty on Social and Economic Rights. It said that no member state should open diplomatic relations with the Taliban and expressed revulsion at the killing of President Najibullah. The Parliament proposed an embargo on all arms supplied to Afghanistan and the suspension of any new aid except for emergency assistance.

However, the Taliban, if they were previously aware of the UN Human Rights Conventions and the importance attached to them as a model for international behaviour, have not given the impression that these weigh anywhere nearly as heavily as their interpretation of the Qur'an and the Shari'a. If anything, they have responded to the condemnations of their policy by interpreting them as attacks by the West, based on Western liberal ideologies, rather than an expression of an internationally held view. The UN and the international community are therefore seen as synonymous with the West.

The Taliban have drawn a distinction between what they term the international and national value systems. One can draw certain initial conclusions about what may be understood by this, but any attempt to try to define the possible differences creates the inevitable risk that one is making gross generalisations. However, at the risk of being shot down, it may be worth very tentatively suggesting possible areas of difference, if only to facilitate what is an enormously complex dialogue.

The Western value system puts a high value on democracy and on individual freedom. Individual freedom is understood to be freedom to seek one's own fulfilment and determine one's own views and perspectives – in short, to give expression to one's own uniqueness. It is contrasted with totalitarian systems in which the state seeks to impose a particular ideology and to control how the individual lives his or her own life.

In the Islamic value system, there is not the same emphasis on individual freedom. The individual is seen as absorbed within, and subject to, society. He or she will identify with the family, tribe, ethnic group, religious group or political party and will generally value conformity with the norms of these groups over personal fulfilment. Energy is more likely to be put into group efforts to improve society than into individual effort to pursue an individual course. There are of course exceptions but, in so far as one is generalising, there is a greater emphasis on society within Islam than there is in the West.

Thus, when the West raises concerns about women not being able to work, the Taliban are surprised that the greatest attention is being given to something that, in their eyes, is not of significance, given the relatively small number of women who have worked in offices. On the other hand, they feel upset that the West has not recognised what they regard as major achievements – the bringing of peace, law and order to Afghanistan and the imposition of a ban on opium production. Similarly, while the West views negatively the imposition by the Taliban of a particular creed on the population, an imposition that is reminiscent of the totalitarian systems it abhors, the Taliban have the conviction that they are improving society through the enforcement of an appropriate moral code.

However, it is not a case of two equal partners trying to understand each other's positions. There is an unequal relationship between the West and the Islamic world based on the greater economic and political power of the former. This leads the West to view the Islamic world with a certain degree of cultural arrogance and a highly critical perspective, which is combined with the somewhat paranoid feelings towards Islam dating back to the crusades to produce a high degree of negativity.

The Islamic world feels resentful at the power the West is able to exert and is particularly paranoid about the all-pervasive influence of Western culture and about the erosion and undermining of indigenous cultures by it. Countries such as Iran take steps such as banning satellite dishes in a vain attempt to stop American television programmes reaching Iranian viewers. The Taliban have gone even farther by banning televisions, although they have cited the Islamic prohibition on the visual representation of the human form as justification.

When the UN makes statements on the basis of internationally accepted Human Rights Conventions, movements such as the Taliban are sceptical. They quite reasonably regard the UN as subject to a considerable degree of influence from the United States, and conclude from this that UN conventions draw heavily on Western values. It should not be assumed that this is a view held only by the Taliban. The threat to Afghan culture, either by Western values or by socialist ones, is felt very keenly by the population, and most Afghans would place a maintenance of their culture very high on their list of life priorities.

It is surprising that the indigenous cultures have survived so well in Afghanistan, given the upheaval created by the conflict. However, other influences have inevitably crept in, particularly amongst the refugee populations in Pakistan and Iran. The success of the Taliban movement also suggests that the phenomenon of religious revivalism that manifests itself so often in situations of conflict or societal trauma is a factor in the consideration of cultural changes in Afghanistan. The existence of so many other movements – such as the Mujahidin – before the Taliban, which have reinterpreted the prevailing culture and religion, may have added to the cultural confusion and uncertainty created by the conflict and made people more inclined to follow a new movement offering certainties in an absolute form. The interest of young people in the Taliban movement is particularly interesting.

At the risk of making further generalisations, it may be useful in the discussion of the interface between the Taliban and the international community to consider some of the more obvious values held by the Afghan population.

Outside the countryside, education is regarded as being enormously important as a means of escaping the stranglehold of poverty. Certainly, in urban areas and refugee communities, every family one meets will put this very near the top of their list of priorities. However poor a family may be, it will struggle to find a way of paying for some kind of education for its children. If family resources are scarce, greater efforts will be made to educate boys rather than girls, but education for girls is still regarded as important. As already mentioned, for many refugee families in Pakistan and Iran the ban on female education by the

Taliban is a significant factor in their consideration of the circumstances under which they would return to Afghanistan. This is inevitably more the case for families from an urban environment.

Other human rights that most Afghans would prioritise include the rights to peace and stability, the right to an adequate standard of living, the right to good health and the right to personal security. The latter includes the right not to be robbed, sexually violated or physically harmed. It is in relation to this particular right that there is the greatest difficulty in considering the policies and practice of the Taliban. On the positive side, they have improved law and order so that people are less likely to be the victims of theft, either in their homes or when travelling, although there have been episodes in which law and order have deteriorated. Further, the Taliban forces have not manifested a tendency to rape and loot in the wake of battle or to abuse women sexually. In this sense, their record is very much better than that of some other elements in Afghanistan. However, they have created a climate of fear in Kabul and Herat by imposing a strict dress code and sometimes beating women and men who do not comply. This has been heightened by the arbitrary behaviour of Taliban forces and their suspicion of those they suspect of having links to the opposition, particularly the ethnic minority groups. Violence caused by anarchy has therefore been replaced by violence sanctioned by religion.

It may also be useful to consider some of the main provisions of the UN Human Rights Conventions and the extent to which the Taliban contravene these. Article 6 of the International Convention on Economic, Social and Cultural Rights of 3 January 1976 states:

> The States Parties to the present Covenant recognize the right to work, which includes the right of everyone to the opportunity to gain his living by work, which he freely chooses or accepts, and will take appropriate steps to safeguard this right.

Article 3 makes it clear that the Covenant applies to women as well as to men when it states:

> The States Parties to the present Covenant undertake to ensure the equal right of men and women to the enjoyment of all economic, social and cultural rights set forth in the present Covenant.

It could be stated, in response to the Convention, that women are still accorded the right to work within the agriculture sector in that such work continues without hindrance. However, women are denied the right to seek employment within the urban environment on the grounds that they may interact with men outside their family. The international community could take the view that it is acceptable, on the grounds of cultural relativism, for women and men to work separately and could seek to explore what flexibility there may be on the part of the Taliban regarding the employment of women on the basis of separation. At present, there is some flexibility in relation to work of a priority nature, meeting health or other urgent needs. The preference is, none the less, that women focus exclusively on their roles as wives and mothers and as educators of the next generation of Muslims. However, opinions are divided in the international community as to whether the separation of women and men is acceptable. Some regard it as yet another form of apartheid.

Article 11 relates to the issue of hardship:

> The States Parties to the present Covenant recognize the right of everyone to an adequate standard of living for himself and his family, including adequate food, clothing and housing ...

Where women have to work because of personal hardship, there is some difficulty. The Taliban argue that the extended family will provide, or the *zakat* system of charity will be used, and that it is never necessary for women to work. However, because of acute poverty, many nuclear families are barely able to survive as a unit, let alone help members of their extended families or their neighbours. With the evidence from Kabul suggesting that extended family or charitable assistance is not always given, agencies have to provide valid arguments to justify such women finding an economic role.

Destitute families in Kabul are also not able to call on their relatives elsewhere. The worsening economic conditions in Iran and the withdrawal of rations in Pakistan, combined with the requirement for refugees to pay for health, education, water supply and electricity, have virtually removed the capacity of refugees to help their relatives in Afghanistan. The severe drought of 2000–2001 has reduced people throughout the country to a marginal level of existence where they cannot easily help others. The return of refugees in large numbers from Iran in the past year or so, under strong pressure from the Iranian authorities, has further reduced the capacity of the population to survive.

Article 13 refers to education:

> The States Parties to the present Covenant recognize the right of every-one to education. They agree that education shall be directed to the full development of the human personality and the sense of its dignity and shall strengthen the respect for human rights and fundamental free-doms ...

It goes on to provide that: 'Primary education shall be compulsory and available to all' and that: 'The development of a system of schools at all levels shall be actively pursued.'

These two parts of the Covenant could provoke different responses from the Taliban. They would, for example, argue that religious educa-tion is provided within the family and that this, in their view, is all that is needed to ensure the full development of the human personality and the sense of its dignity. They would equally argue that Islam does strengthen respect for human rights and fundamental freedoms. How-ever, they are clearly not in agreement that schools are, *per se*, a necessary part of female education. Schools are, in their view, appropriate only if they provide an education that, in their terms, meets the objectives set out in the first paragraph from Article 13. For the Taliban, it is the nature of education that is at issue rather than its availability. However, agencies can, at the very least, reasonably advocate for education to be provided so that women can work in occupations that provide a service to other women.

The Convention on the Elimination of All Forms of Discrimination Against Women of 3 September 1981 states that:

> the term 'discrimination against women' shall mean any distinction, exclusion or restriction made on the basis of sex which has the effect or purpose of impairing or nullifying the recognition, enjoyment or exercise by women, irrespective of their marital status, on the basis of equality of men and women, of human rights and fundamental freedoms in the political, economic, social, cultural, civil and any other field.

There can be no doubt that women are in practice being discriminated against in terms of having unequal access to health and education services. The discussions between the Taliban and international agencies over the summer of 1997 about whether women should be permitted to secure health care only in one hospital, specifically designated for women, did not relate to the principle of whether women are permitted access to health care, which is accepted by the Taliban, but to the possibility that resources might be provided on a much smaller scale to female health care.

While one can draw a clear distinction between the Taliban and others in their treatment of the population at large, it is difficult, at this stage, to compare the state-sanctioned violence perpetrated by the Taliban against prisoners and that of the Soviet period or the period of the Mujahidin government. The Taliban justify their arrests on the grounds that those seized have either acted seditiously, in other words against the interests of the Islamic state, or corruptly.

As indicated above, another difficult question in considering human rights in relation to the Taliban is whether they have gone further than other Islamic governments in introducing a legally sanctioned system of apartheid, albeit on the basis of gender rather than race. Other governments, such as those of Sudan, Iran, Saudi Arabia and Pakistan, have decreed that women and men should be segregated. However, they have varied in the degree to which they have enforced this requirement and also in the degree to which they have relaxed it over time. Of these three, only Saudi Arabia now imposes a high degree of segregation. Pakistan, Iran and the Sudan have largely eased restrictions.

The key question is to what extent the international community should rely on the UN Conventions or, alternatively, take on board the values and perspectives of one or other element of the Afghan population in seeking to engage in dialogue with the Taliban, and how this might modify the position it adopts. Consideration therefore has to be given to whether there are aspects of the UN Human Rights Conventions with which it is unreasonable to expect compliance under present circumstances in Afghanistan. One could, for example, take the view that a society that has experienced trauma at the hands of the superpowers should be allowed the freedom to restore itself through a reinterpretation of old certainties, and that it will then move towards internationally accepted standards. However, this may be viewed by many Westerners as requiring too great a compromise on internationally agreed standards, particularly when women in Kabul are affected here and now by the restrictions imposed by the Taliban.

This is a difficult question, and one the international community may or may not be asking itself. It is primarily the USA and Europe that are giving serious consideration to the issue of recognition of the Taliban as the legitimate government of Afghanistan. It is easy to see why these governments might, on the basis of their own value systems, decide that the policies and actions of the Taliban are unacceptable and that international recognition is not appropriate. It is less easy to understand why the Taliban have been the subject of doubt when so many other regimes, with questionable human rights practices, have been accorded recognition.

On 8 May 1997, the Taliban Voice of Shari'a radio station issued a statement on this point:

> There are dozens and even hundreds of states in the world that do not comply in any way with genuine standards of human rights followed by people in the West. Many cases of executions, imprisonment and violation of human rights can be seen in these countries. Not only is no serious objection made against such states but the countries of the so-called supporters of human rights support these states in various ways.

It could be argued that countries such as the USA may have chosen to disregard the human rights records of governments they have recognised simply because those governments were acting substantially in accord with American interests. The Indonesian government is a good example. One may counter this by stating that the USA has a potential interest in the development of oil and gas pipelines through Afghanistan and in a reduction in both opium production and the training of terrorists there. However, the relative costs of Central Asian oil may prove too high, a reduction in the Afghan production of opium may be offset by an expansion elsewhere in the world and the USA may find some way or other of tackling the training of terrorists in Afghanistan. These interests may not, therefore, weigh as heavily as the gender lobby in the USA and the potential loss of votes if the USA were to recognise a regime that was so explicitly and determinedly reducing women's rights.

The same arguments apply to the European Union. It is therefore the flagrant abuse of human rights – as opposed to the normally covert abuse, such as the torture of prisoners, perpetrated by many countries – that is, perhaps, the major issue in determining the question of international recognition. The Taliban's justification of this human rights violation on the basis of a different moral code, and the apparently unbreachable gulf between this code and the Western value system, lead the USA and the European Union to dig in their heels and feel that they must make a stand. The Taliban, in turn, accuse the West of trying to impose their own values and further polarise the relationship. The tortured history of the relationship between the Islamic world and the West, including the growing tensions between expanding radical Islamic movements in European cities – particularly in France – and their populations, then comes into play as people on both sides agonise over whether they should compromise and, if so, how, or whether they should place further conditions on any possible way forward. The presence of humanitarian agencies and their own tortuous negotiations with the Taliban further complicate the picture, as do the efforts of the regional powers to involve themselves, based on their own interests.

11 The Taliban and Pakistan

The preceding chapters have looked at value systems and the impact these have had on the behaviour of the Taliban, of the population and of humanitarian agencies. However, it would be naive to suggest that behaviour is dictated only by value systems, just as it would be unwise to dismiss the contribution of value systems to historical developments. The self-interest of the many actors on the stage that constitutes Afghanistan is also a major factor.

As explained in Chapter 2, Afghanistan as a country has existed for barely a hundred years. For centuries the cities, towns and villages contained within the present borders have been inextricably linked to the Iranian plateau, Central Asia and the Indian subcontinent through trade, culture, religion, ethnicity and military conquests. Although its mountain valleys have given it a rare degree of isolation and a consequent fierce independence, the fluidity in its history has meant that developments in the wider region have impacted on the political, economic, cultural and religious scene in Afghanistan and leaders of the regional powers have had an interest in determining events there.

When the Soviet troops left Afghanistan in February 1989, Pakistan played an active role in trying to bring the Mujahidin parties, both radical and traditionalist, under a single umbrella. It also brought the parties together in 1992 and thereafter to reach some kind of accommodation that would allow them to govern effectively. Agreement was first reached in Peshawar in April 1992, in the presence of the prime minister of Pakistan and representatives of Iran, Saudi Arabia and the UN, that a 50-person commission, headed by Sibghatullah Mujadidi, would take control of Kabul and prepare the way for the formation of an interim government, to be led by President Rabbani, who would hold office for a further four months pending the formation of an assembly to elect a president for a further two years. Rabbani engineered his way into re-election through a hand-picked gathering held in December 1992, but opposition from the other parties led to heavy fighting in Kabul. This was brought to an end only by the mediation of Hamid Gul, the former head of Pakistan's Inter-Services Intelligence (ISI), who had played a major role in supporting the seven Mujahidin parties during the period of Soviet occupation. Pakistan sponsored a further meeting between the parties in Islamabad on 7 March 1993, at which it was agreed, through the Islamabad Accord, that Rabbani would remain as president for a further 18 months.

While this was going on, Dostam was strengthening his position in the north and developing trade and other links with the newly formed Central Asian Republics. At the same time, Ismail Khan, who had created a semi-independent emirate based on Herat, was building an uneasy alliance of mutual self-interest with Iran. The latter welcomed the stability Ismail Khan had brought to western Afghanistan and the opportunity this provided to facilitate the repatriation of the three million Afghan refugees in Iran. Ismail Khan benefited from the material and other assistance given by Iran, which reduced his dependence on the Jamiat leadership of Rabbani and Masoud, to which he had a certain ambivalence. However, he remained wary of Iran's influence in western Afghanistan increasing unduly.

The collapse of the Soviet Union removed the justification for the USA to continue its programme of support to Afghanistan. Military supplies to the Mujahidin officially ended on 31 December 1991 and the humanitarian assistance programme of USAID came to an end in early 1993. The field was left open for Pakistan to pursue its own interests.

As a semblance of order gradually emerged in Kabul after the months of anarchy that followed the April 1992 assumption of power by the Mujahidin government and the leadership question was resolved through the Islamabad Accord, Pakistan continued to involve itself in discussions with the Mujahidin parties as part of its ongoing efforts to create a strong government in Kabul that would promote Pakistan's interests.

However, Rabbani distanced himself increasingly from Pakistan. The latter, which had always been seen to have placed high hopes in Hekmatyar as a potential leader whose interests would coincide with its own, felt growing disappointment at his inability to present an effective opposition to Rabbani and Masoud.

Pakistan was also becoming concerned that Iran and Turkey were developing strong commercial links with Central Asia and that Iran, in particular, looked set to create an important outlet for Central Asian trade to the Indian Ocean through Bandarabas, thus competing with Karachi. Pakistan's interior minister, Naseerullah Babar, chose to counter this trend, and to demonstrate that Pakistan was also a potential outlet for Central Asian trade, through a daring public relations initiative. With maximum publicity, he travelled across Afghanistan himself, via Kandahar and Herat, in October 1994 and then organised a trade convoy to cover the same route. It was this convoy that the Taliban protected, leading to speculation that Pakistan was lending support to the Taliban.

Pakistan's enhanced interest in strengthening its trade links with Central Asia dated from the emergence of independent states in Central Asia following the collapse of the Soviet Union in 1991. The many subsequent occasions on which Pakistan involved itself directly in the opening up of this route (for example, by working to repair the main highway and facilitating negotiations with the oil companies) were further testament to its interest in the Taliban.

Pakistan has consistently denied backing the Taliban. However, strong circumstantial evidence has led the US and other governments, together with Human Rights Watch, to assert that significant support has been provided by governmental and non-governmental elements within Pakistan. Human Rights Watch, for example, notes that the major offensives undertaken by the Taliban have clearly benefited from sophisticated planning and logistics support and stand in strong contrast to the military encounters that the Taliban have otherwise been engaged in. It does, however, comment that many of the Taliban supporters are former Pakistani military officers and intelligence personnel, such as Hamid Gul, the previous head of Pakistan's Inter Services Intelligence. It states that military supplies are purchased through private companies operated by former Pakistani officers from Chinese sources. The report adds that the Taliban have benefited from their very strong links with the Pakistani radical Islamic party, Jamiat-al-Ulema al-Islami, which has actively recruited for them from amongst the students of their own *madrasahs*.

It was strongly rumoured, when the Taliban first emerged, that the USA had, covertly, worked with Pakistan and Saudi Arabia to support the efforts of the Taliban to achieve a total conquest of the country. The hypothesis put forward at the time was that the USA might see the Taliban as having the potential, using Islam as a foundation, to bring Afghanistan under a single leadership and provide it with stability, and that this would facilitate the construction of oil and gas pipelines across Afghanistan. There was thought to be concern that pipelines might otherwise be built across Iran to transport Central Asian oil and gas to Europe and to other parts of Asia and that this would make Europe vulnerable to a disruption in supply if relations with Iran deteriorated.

When the Taliban entered Jalalabad and then Kabul in September 1996, they took most observers by surprise. All the indications were that the movement had run out of steam, exemplified by its failure to make much headway in its 18-month siege of Kabul. The sudden dramatic turnaround in its fortunes when it captured Kabul again engendered speculation that there was a stronger hand somewhere, providing organisational support and ample supplies. The ready stream of recruits from refugee camps, Afghan villages and religious establishments in Pakistan, ever willing to sacrifice themselves, gave further emphasis.

The international reactions to the capture of Kabul on 26 September 1996 provide interesting insights. On 3 October Pakistan's prime minister, Benazir Bhutto, stated that if the Taliban managed to unite Afghanistan, it would be a welcome development. While indicating that she would like to see the Taliban moderate their gender policy, she said that it was not for her to tell the people of Afghanistan what government to choose. She again denied that Pakistan had provided backing to the Taliban.

On 4 October 1996, Radio Pakistan commented: 'It appears that they [the Taliban] enjoy the full support of the war-weary people who have welcomed the prospects for peace that have now emerged in Afghanistan.' The report went on to express a hope that the Taliban administration would implement the Islamic principles of equality, forbearance, justice and respect for all sections of society, particularly women and children. It added a further hope that the Taliban would not provide any opportunities to those who wanted to malign Islam.

On 2 October 1996, only a few days after the Taliban capture of Kabul, one of the radical Islamic parties in Pakistan, Jamiat-al-Ulema al-Islami, which is headed by Maulana Fazl-ur-Rahman, announced that it had prepared a draft constitution for Afghanistan at the request of the Taliban. This was to be put to the party's executive committee before being sent to the Taliban.

On 12 October 1996, the chargé d'affaires at the Saudi Arabian Embassy in Kabul passed on the congratulations of the Saudi King and expressed delight at the enforcement of the sacred Muhammadan law in Afghanistan and the peace and security that had been restored in most parts of Afghanistan by the Taliban.

Rumours that the USA was sympathetic to the Taliban were, in part, fuelled by a statement on 2 October by the American oil company UNOCAL that it regarded the Taliban's new dominance in Afghanistan as a 'positive development'. It argued that a single government there would bring stability and improve the prospects of proceeding with plans to build oil and gas pipelines through Afghanistan from Central Asia. Such rumours were also generated by the more active diplomacy of the USA in Afghanistan over the previous year or so and by early indications, following the takeover of Kabul, that the USA would seek a meeting with the Taliban. The US government was also reported as saying that it saw nothing objectionable in what the Taliban had done. However, perhaps concerned that an over-sympathetic approach might conflict too brazenly with the wave of international outrage at the gender policies of the Taliban, the State Department issued a statement on 8 October in which it warned the Taliban administration that recognition would be contingent on the rights of women being respected. The spokesman nevertheless said that the USA would seek contact with the Taliban.

The pipeline saga has been an intriguing one. Before the Taliban takeover of Kabul, an Argentinian company, Bridas, obtained the right to extract gas from Turkmenistan's oilfields, but the Turkmen government was then offered a better deal by an American oil company, UNOCAL, and reneged on its agreement with Bridas. The latter took the Turkmen government to court and were competing with UNOCAL to secure the agreement of the Taliban to have the construction rights for the pipelines within Afghanistan. The Taliban signed no binding agreements but tended to favour the Argentinian company out of concern at potential American influence if UNOCAL signed the contract. The oil companies gave out very mixed messages. When the

Taliban took Kabul, UNOCAL made a statement welcoming the take-over and the stability it heralded. However, subsequent statements were more cautious and indicated that the oil company did not consider that there was sufficient stability for the pipelines to be constructed and that it might be some years before this was achieved. However, an agreement signed between UNOCAL, Delta Oil of Saudi Arabia and the Pakistan and Turkmen governments in July 1997 provided for the construction of a gas pipeline connecting Turkmenistan to Pakistan through Afghanistan to commence at the end of 1988. UNOCAL, however, enigmatically commented that it would not start the construction work until there was an internationally recognised government in full control of Afghanistan. Notwithstanding this agreement, the Taliban announced on 28 August that they favoured the terms offered by the Argentinian company, Bridas, and that negotiations were in their final stages for a contract to be signed. Bridas intimated that it might be willing to consider construction under conditions of continuing insecurity. In the meantime, Iran signed an agreement with Turkmenistan in May 1997 to provide for the construc-tion of a pipeline linking Turkmen gas and oil supplies to the Iranian and Turkish networks and thus to Europe. Agreement had already been reached in May 1996 that Kazakhstan would begin exporting oil supplies through Iran, delivering crude oil to Iranian refineries on the Caspian Sea in return for the right to export oil from Iran's Persian Gulf ports. Further progress on negotiations for a possible pipeline route across Afghanistan was inhibited by growing insecurity in northern Afghanistan from May 1997 onwards and by the decision of UNOCAL to withdraw from the consortium with Delta Oil and others in the wake of the US air strikes of August 1998 and in response to a strong lobby by the Feminist Majority organisation in the USA against any contractual arrangements between US companies and the Taliban. The USA was not initially opposed to the agreement signed in May 1997 to transport oil through Iran but, over the past year or so, has tended to favour alternative routes via the Caspian Sea to transport Central Asian oil and gas supplies to Europe.

In spite of Pakistan's efforts to play down its possible links with the Taliban, Interior Minister Naseerullah Babar took on a high-profile role in seeking to mediate between the Taliban and Dostam following the takeover of Kabul and the reversal, at the hands of Masoud's and

Dostam's forces, of the initial successes of the Taliban north of the capital. Pakistan's choice of its interior minister, rather than the foreign minister, as mediator, suggested that Mr Babar had already developed good contacts with the Taliban and further indicated that the emergence of the Taliban at the same time as Mr Babar was dispatching a trade convoy through Pakistan was more than coincidental.

Piecing the bits of the jigsaw together, a possible scenario is that the Taliban emerged as a small spontaneous movement in Kandahar and struck a chord with a population desperate for law and order and for certainty. Their evident popularity would have quickly come to the notice of those outside Afghanistan who saw potential advantage in the stability the Taliban might be able to bring to Afghanistan. Their origins in one of the foremost *madrasahs* in Pakistan would also have found favour among radical Islamic elements in Pakistan's military and intelligence services. Similarly, their Pushtun character would have attracted the attention of fellow Pushtuns in Pakistan's corridors of power.

Pakistan could have reasoned that the Taliban, in restoring society to the condition that traditionally pertained in the rural areas, could quickly build support among the Pushtun tribes of southern Afghanistan. The Taliban were likely to have greater popular appeal than the Islamist parties because they were not seeking to overturn the decision-making structures that had always existed and to replace them with new structures appropriate to political parties. They were also not seeking to impose an alien ideology. Instead, their creed represented a return to the situation that existed before the liberalism of the 1950s turned everything upside down. The Taliban movement also appealed to a certain element among the young, and found no problem finding recruits ready to martyr themselves. Pakistan may have thus felt that the Taliban had a good chance of occupying the Pushtun belt and that, if supported, it could hope to take the rest of the country as Abdur-Rahman had done at the end of the nineteenth century with British support. The stability they could then offer would give Pakistan its twin prizes of access to Central Asian trade and strategic strength against India.

As we have seen, the Taliban were able to draw on particular Islamic movements within Pakistan's borders to recruit young people from *madrasahs* throughout the country, including the Afghan refugee camps,

where a number of radical Islamic and Islamist movements had established such centres of Islamic teaching, many supported with Saudi
funding. This recruitment process was augmented by appeals to tribal
leaders in the Pushtun areas of Afghanistan and to those in the refugee
camps, to send some of their young men to fight. These appeals often
met with a positive response, with families possessing a good number
of sons being asked to spare them for the jihad in return for financial
support from the tribe and an enhancement of their status. The Taliban
movement was therefore able to rely on indigenous support as well as
that emanating from outside the country.

The Taliban were also able to have an impact within Pakistan's
Pushtun population and thus increase the power base of the radical
Islamic and Islamist parties within its borders. The BBC correspondent
in Islamabad reported on 13 October 1996, two weeks after the Taliban
capture of Kabul, that many in Pakistan were worried that the widespread concern over corruption and economic decline in Pakistan might
lead students of Islamic institutions in Pakistan to take inspiration from
the Taliban and play a more active role in the political arena. He said
that the execution of Najibullah and the failure of the Taliban to
negotiate an agreement with Dostam, aimed at the creation of a stable
national government, had even worried those who thought the Taliban
advance on Kabul a positive development. This unease had been manifested in Pakistan's initial haste to reopen its embassy in Kabul giving
way to a more cautious approach to diplomatic recognition.

The US air strikes of August 1998 had, as noted elsewhere, the effect
of radicalising the political environment in both Afghanistan and
Pakistan. The links between the Taliban and the radical parties in
Pakistan such as Jamiat-al-Ulema became much more evident, and the
use of these parties as recruiting grounds for Taliban forces came to be
much more in the public domain. The military coup staged by Pervez
Musharraf in October 1999 had been preceded by efforts on the part
of President Nawaz Sharif to achieve some degree of control over the
use of Afghanistan as a base for the training of terrorists. The Pakistani
government was particularly concerned about the alleged presence, in
Afghanistan, of Pakistanis charged with sectarian killings and other
terrorist acts.

The UN sanctions of October 1999 gave the Taliban grounds for claiming that they were being unfairly targeted by the US government and that the US government was using the UN Security Council as an instrument of its foreign policy. The subsequent sanctions of December 2000 were immediately followed by expressions of solidarity by 40 radical organisations in Pakistan convened by Sami al-Haq, head of the Islamic seminary at Akora Khattack, where many of the Taliban leaders had been trained.

Over the following months, the radical parties appeared to be increasingly flexing their political muscles and there was talk of a growing 'Talibanisation' process within Pakistan, leading many professionals to consider moving to the USA and other parts of the West. A spate of sectarian killings targeted at Shi'as, including high-profile professionals, heightened concerns. Musharraf found himself having to walk a political tightrope between the street power of the radicals and increasing US pressure to rein them in and help address the issue of terrorist training camps in Afghanistan. His task was rendered more difficult by the strong links between elements in the army and the radical parties and by the high-profile actions in support of the radicals by the former head of ISI, Hamid Gul.

The terrorist attacks on the World Trade Center and the Pentagon of September 11, 2001 forced Musharraf to make a decision as to whether to respond to US requests for assistance in relation to possible military action against the Taliban and Osama bin Laden or line up with the radical parties in opposing such action. Perhaps influenced by his own concerns over his relative failure in bringing the radical parties under control, he took the considerable risk of indicating his willingness to cooperate with the US government by, among other things, providing overflying rights and assisting with intelligence. This prompted demonstrations by the radical parties against any support of US military operations in Afghanistan, and the bombing raids launched by the USA on Afghanistan from 7 October onwards dramatically increased the scale of these demonstrations. In spite of these, it agreed to allow US reconnaissance aircraft to operate from bases in Pakistan. Although falling short of permitting combat aircraft to take off from Pakistani soil, this was further evidence of his determination to place himself squarely against the radicals. His simultaneous resort to a substantially increased police presence on the streets of Pakistan's cities, combined

with the arrest of leading members of the radical parties, made it very
clear that he was taking the opportunity that had been presented to
attempt a reversal of the radicalisation or Talibanisation process that
had been gaining momentum.

A key factor in his ability to succeed will be the extent to which the
military action undertaken by the USA will generate new supporters
for the radical parties, a very likely scenario, and whether these also
can be contained. He may also face considerable difficulties within the
military, in spite of the removal of officers with more obvious radical
sympathies, and must, therefore, be highly vulnerable to an internal
coup, possibly combined with his assassination. Given that Pakistan now
has a nuclear capacity, the presence of a radical in the ultimate leadership position will inevitably pose an enormous security threat to India
and could result in nuclear war in the region.

Another possible scenario arising out of the US military action is that
it may be able to create the circumstances in which the Northern Alliance
could, relatively easily, re-capture the non-Pushtun areas of Afghanistan,
namely the north and centre of the country. However, capture of the
Pushtun areas might prove much more difficult and could lead Pakistani
Pushtuns, particularly those in the tribal areas, to lend their support to
the resistance against what would be perceived as a US invasion. A strong
Pushtun belt straddling the border could, in turn, lead to calls that the
North-West Frontier Province should secede from the rest of Pakistan.
Such a move could lead to the fragmentationary tendencies that already
exist within Pakistan being amplified, aggravated by the dominant position exercised by the Punjab. The fact that Pakistan is awash with arms
that found their way into the hands of the population from the large
consignments sent by the USA for the Mujahidin during the 1980s will
increase the risk of civil war breaking out between the component parts
of the country. Already, inter-communal tensions within Karachi have
produced very serious levels of violence over many years.

These events raise the question as to whether the US government is
now having to deal with a situation it had an important role in creating.
As indicated earlier, it sowed the seeds for the emergence of the Taliban
by providing support on a massive scale to a group of radical Islamic
parties exiled to Pakistan, in the context of its strategic objective of
weakening the Soviet Union. These parties were thus enabled to develop

a power base in the refugee camps of Pakistan and to educate and train a new generation of adherents through orphanages, *madrasahs* and Islamic colleges. These educational institutes were the recruiting ground for many of those who volunteered to fight for the Taliban.

In addition, by seeking to keep its initial military assistance to the Mujahidin parties covert, the USA allowed Pakistan to act as a conduit for supplies and so to influence how those supplies were distributed. Pakistan has therefore been strengthened by the USA in pursuing its own strategic interests, which have included a wish to control whoever holds power in Kabul and also to keep the independent-minded traditional leaders under rein.

The USA also has an interest in the creation of stability in the region. With the former Soviet Union in a relatively fragile political and economic state, the USA is inevitably concerned not to have a country on the southern border of the CIS where there are no real controls and where drug production and smuggling, terrorism and the arms trade can be organised with a minimum of constraint. Already, the CIS is the major route for Afghan heroin to travel to Europe. Afghanistan also threatens to destabilise Central Asia if the conflict spills over the Amu Darya, or if opposition groups in Central Asia can be given significant support from south of the border. There is also the question of Central Asia's oil and gas reserves, which need secure outlets to the world's markets.

To what extent, therefore, does the USA bear responsibility for the present situation? If the USA had not provided arms to the seven parties selected by Pakistan, would the outcome of the war have been any different? It is likely that the population of Afghanistan would have harried Soviet troops even without US assistance. Perhaps they would have been less effective than they were, but they had already shown themselves capable of significantly undermining the PDPA regime before outside assistance arrived. Furthermore, only a fraction of the US arms supply was thought to have reached the resistance fighters in Afghanistan. Much of it was, as noted above, said to have leaked in various directions within Pakistan itself, creating a gun culture than had not previously existed (Arney, 1990). The internal factors within the Soviet Union that led to the eventual decision on a military withdrawal may not have been significantly influenced by the military strength of the resistance, even though the poor morale of the Soviet veterans was clearly contributing to the malaise within Soviet society. Whether or not US support made a difference to the war effort, it certainly affected the balance of power within Afghanistan, creating an alternative government based on the Seven Party Alliance and, possibly, having a hand in the creation of a replacement government in the form of the Taliban. In neither case has it been possible for governments to emerge through an electoral process, and all efforts by the UN and others to bring together liberals and technocrats to form a government or to secure the return of the former king, Zahir Shah, have failed. One also has to ask whether radicalism is an inevitable part of the Afghan political process, as manifested in the PDPA regime, the Mujahidin parties or the Taliban, or whether such radicalism appeals to those outside Afghanistan as a means of pursuing particular interests and is therefore strengthened where it would otherwise wither.

In considering the responses of the outside world to what is happening in Afghanistan, it is always safer to talk about elements within each country rather than the government. In Pakistan, the military and intelligence services have tended to dominate policy towards Afghanistan, with the political wing being relatively powerless. Similarly, the radical Islamist parties, particularly Jamaat-i-Islami and, more recently, Jamiat-al-Ulema al-Islami have played a key role in support of the Mujahidin and the Taliban, respectively. There are many in Pakistan, including the government, who profoundly regret the gun culture that has resulted from the Afghan war and that has had a particular impact on Karachi. They argue that Pakistan should cease its attempts to influence events in Afghanistan and give priority to a settlement. Further, the advocates for increased trade with Central Asia and for the construction of pipelines tend to favour a peaceful settlement at the earliest opportunity. However, those with interests in drugs or smuggling will have other agendas and may favour continuing instability. It is beyond the scope of this book to describe and analyse the relationships between the various players. All that one can say for certain is that the complexity of these relationships places almost insurmountable obstacles in the way of those mandated to achieve a peaceful settlement of the conflict in Afghanistan, such as the succession of UN envoys.

The military intervention by the USA has added enormously to the complexity of the situation and makes it even more difficult to predict outcomes. If, as appears to be the case, the USA is seeking to instil such fear into those currently supporting the Taliban that they will withdraw their support and be open to participation in new political arrangements, much will depend on whether its basic assumption is correct. It is equally possible that those who might have been wavering in their support for the Taliban before the military strikes will now line up firmly behind them. It is also very possible that the Taliban will find many thousands of people volunteering to fight for them who would not even have considered this, previously. The fact that the Taliban have close links with Osama bin Laden and that he has taken on even more of an heroic role as a result of the US demonisation of him will greatly enhance the ability of the Taliban to replace all the soldiers who have been killed in US bombing raids. It is thus no longer a question of looking at the relative balance of power of the various populations within Afghanistan in considering possible political outcomes. The outrage that the US attacks has generated within Afghanistan, Pakistan and the wider region have created a totally new dimension and produced a very different set of power relationships from the ones that existed before. The future, therefore, looks very much more uncertain.

12 The Taliban and the Wider Region

Many of Afghanistan's neighbours have viewed with concern the emergence of the Taliban, and some have actively engaged themselves in trying to secure its downfall. Iran was immediately vociferous in its criticism of the Taliban. On 7 October 1996, Ayatollah Ali Khamanei, in a Friday sermon, said: 'In the neighbourhood of Iran, something is taking place in the name of Islam and a group whose knowledge of Islam is unknown has embarked on actions having nothing to do with Islam.' He went on to say that the actions being taken in Afghanistan were what he described as clear examples of reactionary and fanatical moves and of an ignorance of human rights. The ayatollah also accused the Taliban of receiving support from the USA, stating: 'The world witnessed how highly the USA spoke of the group. Not only has Washington not condemned it. On the contrary, it has been supporting the Taliban in its suppression of its rivals.'

Following the Taliban takeover of Kabul, Iran's foreign minister, Ali Akbar Velayati, toured Central Asia and India to stress the need for a ceasefire and for the establishment of a broad-based government. In a statement published by the Iranian News Agency on 15 October, Mr Velayati referred to 'recent remarks by Pakistani officials admitting that the USA, Saudi Arabia and Pakistan supported the Taliban', and said that 'followers of a specific religious or ethnic group cannot impose their will on other groups'. In the statement that followed Mr Velayati's discussions with the foreign minister of Kazakhstan, the two foreign ministers expressed the view that the continuation of military operations between the warring Afghan factions could 'destabilise the situation in the region'.

Like Iran, Russia viewed the Taliban conquest of Kabul with grave concern. On 2 October 1996, President Boris Yeltsin called for a summit meeting of the Commonwealth of Independent States (CIS). His national security adviser said that the victory of the Taliban posed a serious threat to the Central Asian Republics because, he said, it wanted to annex parts of them. It was announced that the presidents of Kazakhstan, Uzbekistan, Kirghizstan and Tajikistan, and the Russian prime minister, would meet in Almaty, the capital of Kazakhstan.

The president of Turkmenistan was the only Central Asian leader who did not agree to take part – Turkmenistan is not a party to the treaty on the collective security of the CIS countries. However, on 14 October, the same day as a meeting with a delegation from the ousted Rabbani government, Prime Minister Victor Chernomyrdin of Russia met with President Niyazov of Turkmenistan. Following the meeting, the president said that Turkmenistan intended to coordinate its activities concerning the Afghan crisis with Moscow. He added: 'We do not quite share the results of the Almaty summit. We believe the conflict in Afghanistan is an Afghan domestic affair.' In the meantime, he noted, one should be 'patient' about differing viewpoints in the CIS. He said that Turkmenistan had good neighbourly relations with the entire Afghan population, including the Taliban, and stated that it would not meddle in Afghanistan's affairs.

At a debate at the UN Security Council on 16 October, the Russian and Central Asian delegates spoke of the threat the fighting posed to their national interests and to the stability of the whole region. The Security Council adopted a resolution put forward by Russia.

On 19 October, President Karimov of Uzbekistan received the president of Pakistan, Farooq Leghari, in Tashkent. The joint statement issued, in which the two leaders called for an immediate ceasefire, peace talks and an arms embargo, was said to contradict the previous position of Karimov who, earlier in the month, had called for support to be given to the leader of the Afghan Uzbek community, Rashid Dostam. President Leghari was accompanied by, among others, Pakistan's minister for petroleum and natural resources. It is therefore likely that the question of Central Asian oil being transported through Afghanistan to a port in Pakistan was discussed. The Pakistani president was reported to have reassured Uzbekistan that the Taliban had no territorial ambitions beyond Afghanistan's borders. In spite of a similar meeting with the president of Kazakhstan, Nursultan Nazarbayer, on 28 October, the Kazakh president issued a warning that the Afghan conflict must not spread beyond its borders.

India also predictably took an anti-Taliban position. On 15 October 1996, the Indian foreign minister announced that India did not intend to recognise the Taliban administration in Kabul and would continue to support the government headed by President Rabbani. He added that, under the conditions of continuing foreign interference in Afghanistan, the official recognition of the Taliban movement would mean consenting to foreign interference.

As the Taliban advanced, three countries, in particular, felt concern: Iran, Russia and India. Iran was not only opposed to the Taliban because of competition over oil and gas pipelines. It also had every reason to fear that a radical Sunni movement might foment trouble in Shi'a Iran, especially in Mashhad, where the shrine of the Imam Reza attracts pilgrims in their millions each year; a massive bomb explosion in the shrine caused horrific casualties on a holy day in June 1994 when it was packed full of people. The large Afghan refugee population in Mashhad provides a potential haven for terrorists, and yet the Afghan population there has remained large for many years while the Taliban have been in power in western Afghanistan and return has continued to be problematic. Afghans who returned from Iran found themselves under criticism from the Taliban for not having fought during the jihad against the Soviet occupation, and many sought refuge for a second time in Iran. This fear of terrorism continued in spite of protestations by the Taliban that they had no wish to export their creed beyond Afghanistan's borders, and had much to do with the efforts the Saudi government and/or Islamic organisations in Saudi Arabia had made over the years to promote Wahhabism in Afghanistan and Central Asia and to undermine Iran.

Earlier in the Afghan conflict, Iran took a strong position against the USA following the assumption of power by the Ayatollah Khomeini in 1979, and was alarmed by the growing US and Saudi involvement in Afghanistan as the war progressed. It sought to strengthen the Shi'a minority in the country and lent support to resistance parties within the Shi'a communities of Afghanistan, encouraging most of them to unite under a single party, Hisb-e-Wahdat. However, when Hisb-e-Wahdat suffered reversals in Kabul at the hands of Ittihad-i-Islami and Masoud's forces, Iran was careful to maintain good relations with the Rabbani regime and this support built up during the year before the Taliban takeover of Kabul. Iran also played a very active role in mediating between the different factions, including the Taliban. A deputy foreign minister, Alauddin Borujerdi, was appointed for this purpose.

Following the Taliban takeover of Kabul, Iran hosted a regional conference in Tehran on 29 and 30 October 1996 to discuss the situation in Afghanistan. Invitations were sent to Russia, India, Pakistan, China, Saudi Arabia and the Central Asian Republics as well as to representatives of the European Union, the UN and the Organisation of the Islamic Conference. Pakistan, Saudi Arabia and Uzbekistan did not attend.

Iran also became concerned at the potential fate of the Shi'a population living in the Hazarajat in central Afghanistan, who had enjoyed a high degree of independence since the Soviet invasion, if the Taliban were to take over the area. This population, in a politically and economically marginal situation under Pushtun control from the 1880s until the PDPA coup and the Soviet invasion provided them with the opportunity to achieve effective local autonomy, resisted the Taliban advance with great determination. It thus disregarded protestations by the Taliban that they would respect the rights of all elements of the Afghan population. However, the attitude of the Taliban towards the Hazaras, which was initially relatively neutral, changed markedly following the disastrous defeat the Taliban experienced in Mazar in May 1997, the blame for which it laid squarely at Iran's door. Thereafter, it was rumoured, large numbers of Shi'as living in Herat and Kabul were rounded up by the police and imprisoned, to prevent them providing support to the opposition forces.

Thus, when the Taliban made a successful attempt on Mazar in August 1998, they sought revenge against both the Hazaras and Iran. As noted above, Amnesty International reported that several thousand Hazaras had been systematically killed during the first three days following the capture of the city. Eight Iranian diplomats and an Iranian journalist were also found dead. Iran responded by placing large troop contingents along its border with Afghanistan but, although there were strong demands for an invasion, those urging caution won the day. These were helped by a mediation effort undertaken by the then UN envoy for Afghanistan, Lakhdar Brahimi, who carried out shuttle diplomacy between Tehran and Kandahar over several days.

It does not appear that Iran has ever received a satisfactory response to its demands for an inquiry into the killings in Mazar, but there has been no subsequent resurrection of the tensions between the two sides. However, Iran has given military support to the opposition forces in central and north-eastern Afghanistan and has also provided a haven for opposition leaders such as the former Mujahidin governor of Herat, Ismail Khan.

Russia's position in relation to the Taliban is less unequivocal than that of Iran. The spectre of radical Islam overwhelming Central Asia has been a feature of Soviet and Russian foreign policy since the early days of the Mujahidin resistance to the PDPA, and this was again stated to be a dominant concern when the CIS leaders hurriedly met after the Taliban takeover of Kabul. However, the picture is much more complex than this and this complexity was a feature of the deliberations that went on within the Kremlin and in the discussions between the leaders.

Turkmenistan, with its crippled economy, is desperate for pipelines to be built that will increase access for its gas and oil to outside markets, and this was manifested in its very cautious reaction to the Taliban takeover. The other CIS states were openly critical of the Taliban but opinions were clearly divided as to whether they should provide military support to Dostam and other members of the northern alliance. The Russian security adviser, Alexander Lebed, was said to have urged Russia to provide support to Rabbani's forces. The secretary of the Russian Defence Council was nevertheless reported on 8 October as saying that caution should be exercised in dealing with the Afghan situation, and that Russia and the CIS should not provide aid to Dostam. In the event, they limited themselves to a strengthening of their own defences to the north of the frontier, including an expansion of the CIS forces, most of which were Russian.

Observers at the time commented that Russia was, in any event, unlikely to involve itself militarily again in Afghanistan. It was noted that the army was poorly equipped and low in morale, and that the newly formed armies of the Central Asian Republics were equally ill-prepared for combat duties. It was felt that, even if military support were provided to Dostam, this could not be guaranteed to hold back any

Taliban advance. There was also ambivalence in some of the Central Asian States as to whether it was in their interest to put themselves in a position of conflict with the Taliban, by backing Dostam, when they needed access through western Afghanistan to expand their trade.

There was, however, reported to be considerable anxiety in Russia that the stated policy of the Taliban of non-interference beyond the borders of Afghanistan could change if they took the whole country, or that elements within the Taliban would encourage and support Islamic movements in Central Asia. A statement by the leader of the Islamic opposition movement in Tajikistan that he did not rule out an agreement with the Taliban, in support of the long-standing Tajik insurgency from Afghanistan, will have done nothing to reassure them.

Other factors prompted Russia's concern at the Taliban presence in Afghanistan. In its public statements, it made much of its fears that the Taliban would advance the spread of radical Islam within Central Asia and so promote a further exodus of ethnic Russians from the Central Asian Republics to Russia, which was not in a position to provide for them adequately.

However, although the Afghan war has left deep scars and was, in the eyes of many, a contributory factor in the demise of the Soviet Union, Russia is anxious for good strategic reasons to maintain control of the northern Afghan border. It is also reluctant to give up the power it used to wield in Central Asia and the Taliban threat provides a good justification for it to maintain an armed presence, together with political and economic influence, in some of the republics, particularly Tajikistan. In addition, the instability created by the Taliban advance puts off the day when pipelines are constructed across Afghanistan to transport Central Asian gas and oil to markets other than Russia, which has enjoyed preferential agreements giving it access to these reserves at well below world market prices.

It is hard to judge to what extent the Russian fear of radical Islam is justified. Certainly the societal crisis, which has affected the region in the wake of the collapse of communism and as a consequence of major environmental disasters affecting the health of millions, provides fertile ground for fundamentalist religion. Saudi Arabia has been seeking to exploit this for years, particularly in the fertile Ferghana Valley between Kirghizstan, Uzbekistan and Tajikistan, where radical movements have operated for many decades and where Christian evangelists are also to be found in force. However, some observers of the region consider that family, tribal and ethnic ties will prevent a strong Islamic movement taking hold.

The peace agreement signed in May 1997 between the government of Tajikistan and the Islamic rebels who held the mountainous east of the country provides a good example of this. In January 1993 a fierce civil war sent refugees from Tajikistan into Afghanistan. Some were accommodated on a desert site near Mazar and others went to Kunduz, which had developed into a centre for Islamic radicals. For several years the rebels launched raids from Afghan territory on CIS troops manning the border between Tajikistan and north-eastern Afghanistan, with backing from Jamiat-i-Islami. With the Taliban capture of Kabul and the ousting of Jamiat from power in the capital, Masoud looked to Tajikistan for support. Both Iran and Russia were keen that such support should be provided and both persuaded their respective proteges, in Russia's case the government and in Iran's case the Islamic opposition, to sign an agreement. Although there is a long way to go before peace can be firmly established, it is of interest that the rebels were willing to compromise with the Russian-backed government when strategic interests dictated it.

The fear that the Taliban will increase the spread of radical Islam within Central Asia presupposes that they have such an ambition, something they have consistently denied. Even if one accepts their denial, this does not of course preclude the possibility that the support currently provided to movements such as the Islamic Movement of Uzbekistan through the provision of a haven to its leadership may not extend, through a splinter group or an element linked to the international radical network, to more active support to radical movements in Central Asia. However, the Taliban creed is not easily transferable to Central Asian societies. In so far as it is very much a reflection the Afghan experience, it is not suited to the more disjointed societies of Central Asia where each republic contains an amalgam of ethnic groups as a consequence of Stalin's forced population movements. Central Asia has also experienced years of secularism and relative gender equality. When the Taliban took power it was possible for rural communities in Afghanistan, which had remained largely intact in the refugee camps, to slip easily back into a highly conservative tradition. However, there have been too many changes in Central Asia for people to be clear as to their original traditions. One could argue that the urbanised radicalism that has taken hold in European cities in response to racism could equally take hold in the relatively urban environment of Central Asia, but the conditions are not the same. The European Russians are no longer in a dominant position in Central Asia and cannot afford to demonstrate racism of the kind that exists in Europe. It will be interesting to see whether the US military action against Afghanistan of October 2001 will now provide a catalyst for the growth of radical Islam within the region.

Afghanistan's immediate neighbours, notably Iran and the CIS, have been very much affected by the transportation of opium and heroin produced in Afghanistan across their territories. Both drugs were already in production in Afghanistan before the Taliban came to power but the production of opium, at least, increased dramatically during the early years of their regime, reaching 4,600 tonnes in 1999. This represented 75 per cent of the global supply. Half of this was grown in the province of Helmand in southern Afghanistan and a further 25 per cent in the province of Nangarhar in the east of the country. The total output fell in 2000, as a consequence of the drought that had taken hold in that year. In July 2000, the Taliban leader, Mullah Omar, issued a decree banning the cultivation of opium and this has taken effect in 2001. Both the UNDCP and Western governments have verified that no opium has been grown this year, but they have expressed concern that the large stockpiles that remain are sufficient to meet the European demand for many years to come. Iran was, for a long time, the major transit route but it has made a major investment in border security and this has led to the CIS becoming increasingly the preferred route, with Tajikistan and Kirgizstan, Kazakhstan and Russia used, in particular.

India has been unequivocal in its continued recognition of Burhannudin Rabbani as the legitimate president of Afghanistan. It has long had a strategic interest in seeking to thwart Pakistan' ambition to create a defensive Islamic bloc stretching from Pakistan through Afghanistan to Central Asia. However, it must equally fear that the Taliban example could upset the delicate relationship between Hindus and Muslims in India, already threatened by growing radicalism amongst both Muslims and Hindus.

The part that Saudi Arabia may have played is also of interest. The Saudi government has been barely visible in all the diplomatic manoeuvring that has taken place in Afghanistan. It is said to concentrate primarily on the creation of cultural development in the form of new mosques, schools, institutes of Islamic learning and religious movements rather than diplomatic activity, but its stamp is evident in the Taliban creed and in the manner in which the Taliban operate. Saudi Arabia saw the opportunity presented by the Soviet occupation of Afghanistan to expand its influence there and it provided significant support to the Mujahidin. It also hoped to counter any influence Iran might have in Afghanistan. Following the Gulf War of 1991, Saudi Arabia responded with anger to the support lent by some of the Mujahidin parties to Iraq and it is said to have shifted its financial support to some of the radical Islamic parties in Pakistan. Notable among these has been Jamiat-al-Ulema al-Islami, which has provided many of the recruits to the Taliban.

Some observers think it unlikely that Saudi Arabia has provided much by way of financial support to the Taliban although it did accord it diplomatic recognition following the first Taliban attempt on Mazar in May 1997, along with Pakistan and the UAE. It is quite possible, however, that funding from non-governmental organisations seeking to promote Wahhabism, and from collections within the mosques of Saudi Arabia and from wealthy individuals there, has been reaching Afghanistan through one channel or another.

The US air strikes on Afghanistan of August 1998 brought the Saudi militant based in Afghanistan, Osama bin Laden, into a much closer relationship with the Taliban and the Saudi government felt that it was no longer tenable to maintain full diplomatic relations with the Taliban while Osama bin Laden remained committed to the removal of US forces from Saudi Arabia, by whatever means. It therefore opted to reduce its representation to that of chargé d'affaires. Relations have since been cool and Saudi Arabia would not have offered much resistance to calls from the USA to sever diplomatic relations completely in the wake of the events of September 11, 2001.

13 Osama bin Laden

Osama bin Laden was a little-known figure on the international stage when, in August 1998, allegations by the USA that he was a suspect in the bombings of the US embassies in Nairobi and Dar es Salaam thrust him to world prominence. A member of a leading Saudi family whose business interests included construction of major hotels and office blocks in Saudi Arabia and the Gulf, he had volunteered to fight alongside the Mujahidin against the Soviet occupation of Afghanistan. In so doing, he was among many others from the Islamic world who saw the Afghan jihad as a cause worth fighting for. He even played a role in recruiting Arab volunteers and is reported to have used his significant personal wealth in support of the resistance movement. He returned to Saudi Arabia in 1990 and was outraged by the decision of the Saudi government to permit the stationing of US forces in the country following the Iraqi invasion of Kuwait later that year. He left for Sudan in 1992 to lend his support to the Islamic revolution being pursued by the Sudanese leader, Hassan Turabi. However, his vocal opposition to the US military presence led to pressures on the Sudanese government from the USA and Saudi Arabia for him to leave and he opted to return to Afghanistan, accompanied by many of his supporters. Thereafter, he continued to campaign to secure the removal of US military bases from Saudi Arabia and the Gulf. The USA claimed that he was responsible for a terrorist attack against a US military housing facility in Dhahran in 1996 in which 19 US servicemen were killed. Thus, when the US embassies in Nairobi and Dar es Salaam were the objects of terrorist attacks on 7 August 1998, he was a prime suspect. Without waiting to build up a body of evidence against him to justify his extradition, the USA immediately demanded that the Taliban hand him over to them. The Taliban responded by stating that they were not prepared to hand over Osama bin Laden to the

USA, insisting that he was not responsible for the bomb attacks. Less than two weeks after the terrorist attacks, the USA opted to used force rather than pursue the legal channels available to them. On 20 August, air strikes were launched on alleged terrorist training camps in eastern Afghanistan and on a pharmaceutical factory in the Sudan where, the USA alleged, Osama bin Laden was producing chemical weapons. The prior evidence that the factory in the Sudan was doing more than producing pharmaceutical goods was extremely shaky, and no subsequent confirmation of such an involvement was provided. The attacks on the alleged terrorist training camps in Afghanistan mostly missed their targets and certainly failed to kill Osama bin Laden. Instead, a number of members of a radical Pakistani party were killed. The Taliban made it clear, following the attacks, that he was subject to their authority, that he would continue to enjoy their hospitality and that they would try him in an Afghan Islamic court if religious leaders believed that there was enough evidence that he had masterminded the bombings of the two US embassies.

The air strikes thus did not achieve their supposed military objective of killing Osama bin Laden and they were widely regarded as a cynical effort on the part of President Clinton to divert public opinion from the Monica Lewinsky scandal. A key hearing at which Monica Lewinsky was giving evidence on her affair with the president took place on the same day.

The strikes did, however, have the immediate effect of raising both Osama bin Laden and the Taliban to heroic status within the Islamic world, particularly among radical elements in Pakistan and the Gulf. Thus the Taliban, who hitherto had been isolationist within the Islamic world, suddenly found themselves having to take a position in response to a military attack on Afghan soil. However, they did not have to look for a policy framework with which to determine their response. Osama bin Laden's clarity with regard to his own perspectives on US foreign and military policy would have given the Taliban leadership an immediate answer. Thereafter, Taliban statements on the role of the USA were indistinguishable from those of Osama bin Laden. However, although Osama bin Laden and the Taliban leadership continued to have a clear position in opposing US policy and actions, the USA failed to provide solid evidence that he had been responsible for the terrorist attacks on the US embassies in August 1998. The Taliban maintained a consistent position in their face-to-face negotiations with US government representatives that they would surrender Osama bin Laden to a neutral Islamic country or submit him to the legal processes existing in Afghanistan if the USA could provide the necessary evidence. The USA rejected this and insisted that he be handed over to them. To strengthen their efforts to secure his surrender, the US government prevailed upon the UN Security Council to impose sanctions on the Taliban in October 1999 that froze all assets held in overseas banks by the Taliban and prohibited flights by Ariana Afghan Airlines outside Afghanistan. These sanctions had no impact on Taliban policy and the Taliban continued to restate their previous position. In response, the USA decided to impose even greater pressure and again prevailed upon the UN Security Council to impose further sanctions. These provided for one-sided arms ban on Afghanistan, thus permitting arms supplies to reach the opposition forces but denying them to the Taliban. This was clearly targeted at Pakistan and followed statements by the US government that it had good reason to believe that Pakistan was providing military support to the Taliban. The sanctions also placed even greater restrictions on air communications between Taliban-controlled Afghanistan and the outside world by prohibiting any flights from taking off for Afghanistan or landing, having departed from Afghanistan.

Both sanctions underlined the difficulties that the UN faced in having to play several distinct roles. Thus, as well as having responsibility for the provision of humanitarian assistance to the population of Afghanistan, it was also engaged in seeking a peaceful outcome to the conflict, through the mediation role of the UN secretary-general's special envoy on Afghanistan, in monitoring and reporting on human rights abuses through the UN rapporteur on human rights and in acting as the vehicle, through the UN Security Council, for the expression of the international community's concerns. The UN secretary-general has himself acted as a vehicle for such concerns, issuing statements in response to alleged human rights abuses committed by the Taliban.

The sanctions put in place in December 2000 would appear to have had a significant effect in further radicalising the political environment in Afghanistan. The US air strikes and the earlier sanctions had already led to an immediate increase in the number of Afghans seeking asylum in the West, arising from an increased climate of fear and threat for moderates and intellectuals as a result of the build-up of support for Osama bin Laden and the Taliban. The hijacking of an Ariana Afghan Airlines plane to London in February 2000 was one manifestation of such a trend. However, the sanctions of December 2000 led the rate of arrival of Afghan asylum-seekers in the UK, at least, to almost double. The destruction of the giant Buddhas of Bamyan in February 2001 was further evidence that the Taliban movement had moved into a position where it had almost complete disregard for how the outside world perceived it. The UN secretary-general had been aware of this accelerating radicalisation trend prior to the sanctions of December 2000 and had expressed his strong opposition to the sanctions. He was joined by humanitarian agencies that argued that further sanctions would push the Taliban even more into a corner in which they would have, as their only reference point, the volunteers who were fighting alongside them from other parts of the Islamic world, including Osama bin Laden. It became evident that the radical Islamic Pakistani party, Jamiat-al-Ulema al-Islami, was becoming increasingly influential over the Taliban leadership. Moderate elements within the Taliban appeared to be marginalised and to have very little say over policy. Following the sanctions of December 2000, forty radical parties in Pakistan came together under a single umbrella, at the initiative of Sami al-Haq, the head of the Islamic seminary at Akora Khattack where Mullah Omar and many other Taliban members had been students. There were indications that decision-making within the Taliban was increasingly the domain of a tiny elite and that enormous influence was wielded by Osama bin Laden, by Sami al-Haq, by Fazl-ur-Rahman, the leader of JUI and by Pakistan's intelligence services. Hamid Gul, former head of the ISI from the period of the Soviet-backed government, who had played a major role in mediating between the Mujahidin parties from 1992 to 1996 during the period of the Mujahidin government, has again been very much in the public eye. He has thus made statements in support of the Taliban and been critical of the policy of the Musharraf government. The interlinkages between radical elements in Pakistan and the Taliban are, therefore, extremely strong.

It is thus the case that, within this large network, the ideological underpinning exists for a strongly anti-US position and that Osama bin

Laden, as an important source of inspiration for this network, could, theoretically, have had a role in relation to the terrorist attacks on the US embassies in Nairobi and Dar es-Salaam, on the USS *Cole* and on the World Trade Center and the Pentagon. However, there are very many others in the Islamic world who could equally have had such a role and it is, therefore, incumbent on the USA, as with other legal proceedings, to provide the necessary evidence to prosecute their case against him.

It is of interest that, prior to the terrorist attacks of September 11, 2001, the USA had been engaging more constructively with the Taliban than had been the case under the Clinton administration. The Bush administration had, in particular, responded to Taliban complaints that the international community had ignored the ban imposed by the Taliban leader in July 2000 on opium production. Having verified that the ban had been implemented, the US government, through a statement issued by the US secretary of state, Colin Powell, in May 2001, indicated its welcome of the ban. The USA had also stated that it was reviewing its policy on Afghanistan and that, as part of this, it was engaging in regular discussions with the Taliban. It was clear from the various statements made that the US government was extremely concerned at the growth of radicalism in both Pakistan and Afghanistan. It was, as a consequence, making definite efforts to bolster the Musharraf regime by supporting the provision of World Bank funding to help ease Pakistan's indebtedness. At the same time, it was, prior to the attacks, planning to send in experts on border control, counter-terrorism and money laundering to Pakistan, to strengthen its capacity to weaken the radical parties. This was provided for under a resolution issued by the UN Security Council in July 2001 pursuant to the UN sanctions of December 2000 through which it agreed to recommendations made by a committee of experts commissioned to advise on how the sanctions could be better enforced. The radical parties in Pakistan who are part of the umbrella group set up by Sami al Haq immediately stated that they would do all in their power to block the efforts of those despatched to monitor border controls.

It is difficult to second guess what the outcome of the policy review being planned by the USA would have been if the attacks of September 11 had not happened. Would they have pursued a policy of

constructive engagement with the Taliban aimed to soften their radicalism and to strengthen moderate elements within the movement? Would
they, at the same time, have sought to persuade the Taliban to cooperate
with efforts initiated by the former king, Zahir Shah, to convene the
traditional national assembly, called in times of crisis and known as a
Loya Jirga, to agree on a peaceful outcome to the conflict? The USA
may have hoped that, by weakening the Taliban through efforts to
reduce the human and financial resources available to them, they might
have been able to increase the pressure on them to cooperate.

It is, however, possible that the US government was looking for an
opportunity to overthrow the Taliban and replace it by an alternative
government arising out of a Zahir Shah-sponsored Loya Jirga process
and that the events of 11 September provided such an opportunity. If
that was the case, they must have estimated that they would be able to
deal with any political fall-out in Pakistan arising from such a military
intervention – or they may have disregarded such a potential fallout in
their concern to tackle the radicalisation process that was already
seriously threatening the stability of the regime. There was certainly
no shortage of cogent arguments being expressed in the British media
against military intervention: that this would produce another generation of people seeking martyrdom through attacks on US or other
Western targets; that it could bring down the Musharraf regime in
Pakistan and replace it by a radical Islamic one with a finger on the
nuclear trigger; that the US military would be no match for the Taliban
forces prepared to fight to the death of the last man; that military
action would further radicalise the political environment and produce
many thousands more volunteers to replace those killed in military
action; that the threat of military action had already brought aid
programmes to a halt and led to a cessation of food supplies to millions
of Afghans already at risk of starvation after two years of drought;
that the US military would have to bring in all its own supplies, including water, because of the severe drought; that warnings had been
issued by Russian military with previous experience in Afghanistan
that any military intervention would be extremely high risk; that this
would be another Vietnam, resulting in high casualties and no positive
outcome; that US forces would be highly vulnerable to guerrilla warfare
and suicide attacks. One can only conclude, therefore, that the US

administration was extremely focused on using Osama bin Laden as a hate figure to enable it to pursue wider economic and political goals and that, however cogent the arguments against military intervention were, it did not want to hear them.

14 Conclusions

The Taliban movement has represented an important phenomenon in recent international relations and with implications that go much wider than Afghanistan. Through its extreme radicalism, it has taken on a symbolic role in confronting the dominant position of the USA. By its assertion of an alternative value system and its uncompromising determination to impose this value system on the entire country at the expense of any material benefits that might accrue from a greater level of engagement with the international community, it has made itself almost invulnerable to Western pressures. With the governmental and service infrastructure in a state of collapse and the economy at an extremely basic level, it has created a situation in which it has very little to lose from military action by external powers. This, combined with the potential it has to galvanise anti-US sentiment among the populations of both Afghanistan and the wider Islamic world and the freedom it has, as a non-participant actor in the international community, to provide a haven for guerilla and terrorist movements, has given it enormous power. This power is based on the fact that it is able to build on grievances felt in various parts of the Islamic world with regard to the policies and actions of certain governments. These include the perceived imbalance in the support given by the USA to Israel as against the Palestinians; the willingness of Saudi Arabia and the Gulf states to permit the stationing of US and UK military forces on their soil; the repressive methods used by Russia in response to political demands by the Chechen population who happen to be Muslims and consequent rebel activity; the authoritarian nature of the Uzbek government and its unwillingness to engage constructively with Islamic organisations; the harsh methods used by the Chinese government in suppressing rebel activity from within the Uighur Muslim population in western China. It is also able to draw on the growing power of the radical parties in Pakistan, which is, in turn, a response to the high levels of corruption and elitism that has been so manifest in Pakistan since its inception. Thus, although the movement may, in practical terms, have depended heavily on elements within Pakistan for its survival, it has also been in a strong position to echo and act as a catalyst for the grievances felt by huge populations. Were this not the case, the Taliban regime could have been regarded as simply another regime isolated from the international community with an unacceptable human rights record. It would have thus joined countries such as Cuba, Burma and the previous Khmer Rouge regime in Cambodia as international pariahs regarded as marginal to internationally held priorities. However, the Taliban have been able to confront criticisms of their gender policies and of their treatment of ethnic minorities by presenting the USA, in particular, and the major players on the world stage, generally, as often guilty of human rights abuses of significant magnitude.

The international community can obviously respond by seeking to marginalise the Taliban and similar movements as extremists. However, it has become clear following the terrorist attacks on the World Trade Center and the Pentagon that western governments have not been effective in infiltrating terrorist networks and pre-empting attacks. It has also become clear that there will be no shortage of people in the Islamic world who are willing to martyr themselves for as long as there are legitimate grievances against the US and other governments. It is encouraging that, as a result of the attacks of 11 September, the USA has begun to reflect on its policy in relation to Israel and the Palestinian Authority with a view to redressing the imbalance although it is far from clear that they will tackle this in more than a tokenistic way. It is also positive that the Musharraf regime in Pakistan has taken active steps to tackle corruption and so deal with one of the major grievances of the radical Islamic parties. However, the US government, in particular, must go further than this and also address the arrogance and insensitivity that are a consequence of its overwhelming position of power and which, as much as its policies, upset moderate opinion in many parts of the world. Regrettably, examples of this arrogance and insensitivity have been all too evident in the statements that the US government has made since it commenced its bombing raids on targets in Afghanistan on 7 October 2001. The outrage over the bombings that has been felt throughout the Islamic world has been dismissed as secondary to the security concerns of the USA. The deep-seated Islamophobia that has come to the surface as a result of the events of September 11 and has manifested itself in and hate mail directed at and attacks on individual Muslims, mosques and organisations identified with Islam and Afghanistan has also to be addressed. The action already taken by the US and UK governments in this regard must be welcomed but it is also important to reflect on the role of the media, particularly in the USA, in reinforcing a myopic perspective by virtue of the very limited coverage of the situation in other parts of the world. There is a very obvious danger, as a result of these events, that the US and other Western governments will, through their statements, further reinforce the climate of fear that has been generated and that they will present the world beyond Europe as threatening, "uncivilised" and unsophisticated. In fact, it may actually suit some interests in the USA to use such images for the very purpose of maintaining such fear, in order to justify a much increased level of defence expenditure in support of globalisation.

Events since August 1998 in Afghanistan have demonstrated that what are perceived as hostile acts by the USA, acting alone or through the umbrella of the UN Security Council, have the effect of further radicalising the political environment. Such radicalism has manifested itself both in actions that may be regarded as anti-Western and anti-Christian and those that could be characterised as representing an ultra-conservative perspective, such as the destruction of the great rock-face Buddhas in Bamyan in February 2001. There is a distinct danger that the events of September 11 will produce a similar radicalism among the US population, which will necessarily influence government policy. This may manifest itself in increasing isolationism, Islamophobia, growing racism, increased prejudice and violence against minorities and a growth in religious revivalism – in other words, the policies and practice of the Taliban could begin to be echoed, albeit in a very different form, within the USA itself.

It is, therefore, very much in the interests of the American people that actions are taken by its government that seek to address both the legitimate concerns of moderate elements within the Islamic world and Americans' own relative ignorance as to what is happening in the world beyond the USA. It did look for a few weeks following the events of September 11 that the US government might pursue such a course, but the military action that commenced on 7 October made it very clear that the US government had opted to go down the road of continuing warfare against a hate figure in the Islamic world. The implications of this approach for the whole world are potentially terrifying.

Bibliography

Arney, George, 1990, *Afghanistan*, Mandarin, London.

BAAG (British Agencies Afghanistan Group), 1997, *Return and Reconstruction*, Refugee Council, London.

Dupree, Louis, 1980, *Afghanistan*, Princeton University Press, Princeton, NJ.

Guillaume, Alfred, 1956, *Islam*, Penguin, Harmondsworth.

Halliday, Fred, 1995, *Islam and the Myth of Confrontation*, I.B. Tauris, London.

Hiro, Dilip, 1988, *Islamic Fundamentalism*, Paladin, London.

Hopkirk, Peter, 1990, *The Great Game*, John Murray, London.

Rashid, Ahmed, 1994, *The Resurgence of Central Asia: Islam or Nationalism?*, Zed Books, London.

Roy, Olivier, 1986, *Islam and Resistance in Afghanistan*, Cambridge University Press, Cambridge.

Rubin, Barnett, 1995, *The Search for Peace in Afghanistan: From Buffer State to Failed State*, Yale University Press, New Haven, CT.

Ruthven, Malise, 1984, *Islam in the World*, Penguin, Harmondsworth.

Save the Children Fund UK, 1994, *Report on Herat Programme*, SCF-UK, London.

Yuval-Davis, Nira, 1997, *Gender and Nation*, Sage, London.

Index